More praise for *Faith & Fitness*

"Tom Hafer's understanding of the spiritual responsibility we have toward care for the land is clearly in line with . . . biblical teachings as caretakers (not exploiters) of the earth. . . . *Faith & Fitness* outlines the link between caring for the land that produces our food and the effects the food produced on the land will have on our bodies."
—Stan Doerr, executive director/CEO, ECHO, Inc.

"*Faith & Fitness* demonstrates three changes that can result in faithful and happy lives. First is a shift away from money toward love as the primary motivator for our actions. Second is the move away from a need-to-lose-weight model toward one focused on the need to feed others. Third is the shift to honor our bodies so as to care for others. Packed with practical information and advice about eating and exercising, this down-to-earth book helps us move toward compassionate faith. Hafer's claim is that it will also make us both spiritually and physically more healthy!"
—Shannon Jung, professor at Saint Paul School of Theology, Kansas City, and author of *Sharing Food* and *Food for Life*, both from Fortress Press (2004, 2006)

"*Faith & Fitness* puts in perspective that being healthy and fit is more than exercise and nutrition. You need to be spiritually fit as well. This book creates an awareness of the daily requirements we need to be healthy physically and spiritually. The book has inspiration with perspiration!"
—Lance Shore, vice president, sales and marketing, Torque Fitness

FAITH & FITNESS

DIET AND EXERCISE FOR A BETTER WORLD

TOM P. HAFER

Augsburg Books

MINNEAPOLIS

Large-quantity purchases or custom editions of this book are available at a discount from the publisher. For more information, contact the sales department at Augsburg Fortress, Publishers, 1-800-328-4648, or write to: Sales Director, Augsburg Fortress, Publishers, Box 1209, Minneapolis, MN 55440-1209.

Library of Congress Cataloging-in-Publication Data
Hafer, Tom P., 1967-
   Faith & fitness : diet and exercise for a better world / by Tom P. Hafer.
      p. cm. — (Lutheran voices)
   Includes bibliographical references.
ISBN-13: 978-0-8066-5331-0
ISBN-10: 0-8066-5331-0 (pbk. : alk. paper)
   1. Stewardship, Christian. 2. Food—Religious aspects—Christianity. 3. Physical fitness—Religious aspects—Christianity. I. Title. II. Title: Faith and fitness.
   BV772.H165 2007
   248.4—dc22   2006030590

Cover design by The DesignWorks Group, Charles Brock; Cover photo © Thomas Brostrom and Dusan Jankovic. Used by permission.
Book design by Michelle L. N. Cook

The paper used in this publication meets the minimum requirements of American National Standard for Information Sciences—Permanence of Paper for Printed Library Materials, ANSI Z329.48-1984.

Manufactured in the U.S.A.

11   10   09   08   07   2   3   4   5   6   7   8   9   10

Contents

Introduction

I often think of just how lucky I was to be put in such a unique position. My career path wasn't of my choosing, but looking back, I realize that I was exactly where I needed to be.

At twenty-two years old, I started a physical therapy clinic that did well. It was to be a sports medicine clinic in southern Florida. Its purpose was to care for high school, collegiate, and community athletes, as well as high-profile professional athletes with vacation homes in the area. What I ended up with was a large clinic full of senior citizens whose goals and abilities had nothing to do with athletics. Instead, they were concerned with functional activities, such as strengthening their legs to get out of a chair or walking up stairs. Those were the people with whom I worked. It wasn't the NBA or the NFL, but simply senior citizens who wished to learn to walk again. I didn't intend it that way. It was just the way my last two decades panned out.

After physical therapy school, I had even taken an additional two years to receive my Athletic Training Certification (A. T., C.) in order to become more marketable in the community as a sports medicine provider. In the early years, I would ask myself, "Why did I spend all those years in college for sports medicine when I am working with the elderly?"

Although it wasn't my design, the work became fairly lucrative. Services for seniors were in high demand, and they paid accordingly. So while some of my former sports medicine classmates were in exciting careers with universities and a few professional sports teams, I was working hard with seniors in my little corner of the Sunshine State.

Like most young Americans fresh out of college, I followed the dream of working and earning my fortune. I worked hard. Nothing could slow down my drive to achieve. Despite the success, something was missing. My diet was poor. My once disciplined exercise routine was now sporadic. Imagine—a guy who studied nothing but exercise and nutrition was neither exercising nor eating well! I had (and still have) a wonderful wife, three incredible children, a large home, and that successful business. But, at that point, my spiritual life was feeble. My life wasn't drastically wrong or evil, just out of balance.

I have the senior citizens to thank for my early success. After all, they trusted in me, which is why they came for physical therapy. But I was entrusted with something more than their bodies. In addition to receiving medical services, they told me their stories, and it was the stories they shared that eventually made an impact. Out of all age groups, it seems that the elderly communicate through stories most often. Initially, I took the stories they shared with me at face value. There was variety in the joys and sorrows, regrets and accomplishments they shared, but one lesson was the common thread present in some form in every account. Stories of thousands of older adults told me again and again what I, an ambitious young person, needed to hear: Don't be a fool. Out of love and concern, they were warning me to find my balance; to treasure what I have that matters most and not be a fool. "For where your treasure is, there your heart will be also" (Luke 12:34).

There are moments when God speaks. Oftentimes the voice is so subtle that we choose to ignore it. If we listen, truly listen, it is usually such a profound revelation that the very patterns of our lives are shaken and the paradigms shift. Such a revelation came to me on December 15, 1997.

I had just sold my physical therapy clinic. I turned a profit and quickly started my plans to do it all over again. I faced long and disciplined hours. It was then that my four-year-old son, Daniel, received a five-dollar bill in the mail from his great-grandmother. As I was leaving for work that morning, I noticed Daniel holding his crisp bill tightly. At that time, my wife was the one who kept things organized and made sure the needs of our three children were met. I didn't have time for such things—after all, I was the successful breadwinner. But that morning I decided to make a promise to Daniel: to come home early and take him to the store to spend his five dollars. As I left, I couldn't help but wonder what he would decide to get. After all, five dollars is big money for a preschooler. He loved candy and could get a lot of it for that. But maybe he would want a water pistol.

Throughout the day, I continued to wonder what Daniel's mystery purchase would be. I was proud of my plan to take valuable time out of my important business schedule to drive him to the store to spend his gift money. At 5:30 P.M., I walked into my home and was greeted by my preschool son descending the stairs, smiling slightly, and trying hard to contain his enthusiasm. With his hand outstretched and clutching the five-dollar bill, Daniel said, "Here, you take this money, Daddy. Then you won't have to work so much."

Soon after that we sold the big house, took our first real family vacation, started eating healthily and exercising regularly. I began working only forty hours a week. Within a few years, we relocated our home in order for me to attend seminary. My goal was to gain a deeper understanding of God's hope for me—never to be disillusioned again.

> I went to the woods because I wished to live deliberately, to front only the essential facts of life, and see if I could learn what it had to teach, and not, when I come to die, discover that I had not lived. . . .[1]
> —Henry David Thoreau

What a horrible tragedy—to reach the end of life discovering that accomplishments one pursued were left wanting. I learned this lesson in time, and my hope is that you will learn it, too. Think of this as a financial self-help book with a goal of exposing the shortcomings of material pursuits to the exclusion of healthy self-fulfillment. While it is obviously a book about fitness—emphasizing disability-free living through diet and exercise—another goal of this book is to help you realize the value of community.

But, most importantly, I hope you find this to be a book that offers a balance between fitness and wealth that leads to a longer, more fulfilling life of socially responsible Christian discipleship. I realize that these hopes are tall orders for one thin publication. But you will see that through dynamic paradigm shifts that lead to a more simple life, both fitness and wealth will find their proper places in your community of family and friends—as well as in the world.

I warn you that this publication will not teach you the steps to be rich. You will not learn tricks for quick weight loss, and it won't help you find a better career, get a bigger house, or look younger. There are plenty of books that can help you with those things.

Rather, this book should convince you that the rabbit trails we chase to improve our looks, our wealth, and our position all fail to provide us with the fulfilling life of a servant. Each chapter you read will include a couple of questions to ponder to stimulate your thinking about how you can apply this information to your life in concrete, practical ways. Talk the questions over with family, friends, and even members of a study group at church.

Together we can respond to God's call to be good stewards of our own health, our neighbors' health, and the health of our planet. May the stories you tell as a senior be joyful, colorful, and of good health!

Chapter 1: The Way

"The Way" was one of the names for the original Christian community in the first century A.D. The term described this new way of treating people with compassion and love, as a Nazarene named Jesus taught.

The Cross

Jesus can be admired for his miracles, exalted for his leadership, even worshiped for his provocative teachings, but it is his cross that changes us. The cross embodies this paradoxical understanding of a life worth living: by losing your life, you will save it. It is living life, not in cut-throat competition with your neighbor, but in service to your community. It is telling the world that all that it strives for—physical beauty, success, fame, or riches—means nothing compared to life as a servant in God's grace. Although we may admire Jesus for this or that attribute, we can't completely embrace God's will, God's way, God's values, and God's grace until we examine the question, "Why the cross?"[1]

We know that it is through faith in Christ that we are made righteous, and there is nothing in our power that we can do to earn our way to salvation. Christ has already paid the price for our sin, and we each are made a new creation through the resurrection. Because of this, we can rest knowing that God will never abandon us.

The cross symbolizes Christ's sacrifice then and now, exposing the truth of our own natures and also of God's great love. If we embrace the cross and the promise it has for us, we can begin to understand the deeper richness of its meaning. After all, Jesus says that he is the poor today.[2] He is today's "crucified people, the least of these" (Matthew 25:31-46). The least of these include the poor, hungry, thirsty, neglected children and seniors, political casualties, and all those who are ignored or forgotten. Because Jesus identifies with suffering people, when we neglect those who suffer, we are abandoning Jesus on the cross once again.

A life of service in God's grace is a flip-flop from a life of self-service. God's desire is for us to take up our own cross and follow the leader into action and proclamation of the good news. In losing your life, you really will save it. The cross establishes not only the extent to which God loves us, but also just how far we are to go in our faith and discipleship in response to God's love and favor—to the best of our human ability. By extending love to the least of these, we extend the love that Christ showed us on the cross. Still, it is most important to emphasize the primacy of faith over works. We are called by Christ to love one another, and it is our faith in him only, and not the good works we do, that gives us new life. We do good works because we are moved with compassion by Christ's sacrifice on the cross. We do not do good works to earn salvation; we are not able to do such a thing. Faith in Christ makes us a new creation. Our salvation is free; the price has been paid already.

This book has a very specific purpose: to put our lives into perspective regarding health. Take a step back and view the big picture. Like most people of affluent societies, we have the luxury of never being malnourished. Yet, like most people of affluent societies, we have the pain of weight problems or poor health as a result of inappropriate diet and lack of exercise. Typically, when we speak of our personal wellness, we don't think in terms of Christian compassion and love. Yes, we may say we "love to be thin," "love to live long," or "love to be healthy," but we'd never put the idea of love in the same sentence with Christian mission and personal health. Yet, Christ invites and empowers us to care for ourselves so that we can better care for others.

Regarding food, God structured creation with all the provisions and nutrition a person needs for a healthy and full life. Ironically, we who are privileged spend millions each year on diet aids, appetite suppressants, and medical intervention for problems with obesity while the least of these still go hungry. The epidemics of both obesity and world hunger continue to exist together in the same global community, killing huge numbers on both sides.

Regarding exercise, unlike everything made by humans, the body rebuilds and improves itself with consistent, moderate to heavy use, and weakens when not in use. Our bodies were created to move, work, and exercise.

Ultimately, the sacrifice Jesus made on the cross and the words he spoke shape our own existence and purpose. We can trust God's natural design for a healthier way to find personal, communal, and global wellness. When we consider our desire for better health or weight loss, let us clear our minds of old ideas and struggles, start at the cross of Jesus—hungry, thirsty, open, and broken—and go from there.

Questions to Ponder

What does the cross teach about the nature of God's love? How does my faith in Christ shape my daily decisions?

Community

> Day by day, as they spent much time together in the temple, they broke bread at home and ate their food with glad and generous hearts, praising God and having the goodwill of all the people. And day by day the Lord added to their number those who were being saved.
>
> —Acts 2:46-47

We learn all about The Way[3] throughout the book of Acts in the New Testament. As with any community, that first-century group of believers had trials and struggles amid their "acts." The most revealing piece of the picture we get of those original Christians is that a Christian didn't function as an individual, but only as a member of a community. In other words, when the individual was in good fortune, the whole community benefited, and when the individual was in need, the entire community was there to respond by sharing. "Now the whole group of those who believed were of one heart and soul, and no one claimed private ownership of any possessions, but everything they owned was held in common" (Acts

4:32). This was the original design of the Christian movement—collective good will for all.

Being of one heart and soul helped the original
Christian community to collectively bring the message
of God's revelation through Jesus Christ to the global
Christian religion it is today. With unity of purpose, they
offered support to each other. "There was not a needy
person among them" (4:34). This way of caring for each
other was alien to the people of the Roman Empire; it
was noticed and found to be attractive to some . . . and
then more. The Way added numbers to their mission
every day. The original community grew dramatically,
without force, but with gentleness and compassion. So,
salvation spread quickly and continues to spread, not
with force, but with the opposite: compassion. Compassionate unity like that lived among the original Christians is the model that has kept the Christian movement
strong throughout the last two thousand years. Christian communities in communist Eastern Europe and the
old Soviet Union, as well as in China today, survived
in large measure because of the strength that emerged
from that original Christian community. But the success
of that compassionate, loving model should be no sur-
prise to us, since it is, after all, how Christ asked us to
treat one another—with love.

The Christian community best serves Christ and
humanity by carrying a towel for foot washing or food
rations rather than a sword or gun. In fact, historically,
when this original Christian community model of compassion has been neglected, the spread of Christianity
has wavered—most notably during the Crusades and the
Inquisition. The harder we try to force the values of The

Way, the less authentic it becomes. It is the theology of the towel (Jesus washing the feet of the disciples), and not the victory of soldiers dressed in armor that is the heart of Christian outreach. As Jesus' arrival in Jerusalem on a donkey demonstrated, a greater power is shown through human weakness. While the world waited for a powerful ruler to defeat the Roman oppressor through force, Jesus conquered as the servant. The cross established the greatest strength through human weakness.

The power of the community, as it is understood in the book of Acts, echoes in the twentieth century, despite that century's reputation for bloody conflicts. Behind the difficulties of the last century, there are glimpses of individuals who brought to life Christ's model of compassion for humanity. Four key people who spoke and acted for the good of the community at large—and so, changed the world—are Desmond Tutu, Nelson Mandela, Gandhi, and Martin Luther King Jr.

The African word *ubuntu* means to formulate an identity only in relation to the community, and not as an individual.[4] Archbishop of South Africa Desmond Tutu understood the community through *ubuntu* and so helped the stable movement from a divided South Africa to a unified South Africa, ending apartheid in 1994. Then, Nelson Mandela was elected president of South Africa after twenty-seven years as a political prisoner. Through his leadership and vision, the Truth and Reconciliation Commission (TRC) was formed in 1994, and harmony began to be restored among these African peoples. Forgiveness by the black South Africans of their brutal white oppressors was possible. The power of a peaceful movement of the whole community freed all people from the oppressive rule of apartheid. Bloodshed was largely avoided and a relative peace emerged through forgiveness without retaliation. Nelson Mandela and Bishop Desmond Tutu taught the world that forgiveness is a supremely Christian virtue, a conscious choice. Unless it is conferred on others without demanding anything in return, it is not genuine.[5] By serving the needs of the whole community, forgiveness established a greater, permanent victory through peace and not bloodshed.

For fifteen years, Martin Luther King Jr. worked to build a community of peace in the United States. Dr. King understood the value of all members of the community, black and white. "We shall overcome" became the nonviolent anthem of protest sung by the community, all races standing against the inequalities of segregation. Dr. King, a Baptist minister, was greatly influenced by Mohandas Gandhi, a Hindu. It was from the success of Gandhi's actions that Martin Luther King Jr. learned the true value of nonviolent resistance. In the process of serving the whole community, Dr. King enriched the very way people strive for peace—for all. As Christ demonstrated, once again power was shown to be greatest through compassion, not oppression.

Mohandas Gandhi led India to independence by living out his understanding of community and nonviolence. He was greatly influenced by Jesus' teachings, specifically his Sermon on the Mount (Matthew 5:1–7:29), and the writings of the Christian Russian novelist, Leo Tolstoy. Part of Gandhi's success involved the building of communities throughout India. The members of each community shared all tasks and supported one another in a *swaraj* (self-rule) fashion.[6] It was this self-rule understanding that Gandhi wished for all of India, based on Jesus' model. Such a national community that was self-supportive and supportive of each member reflected Christ's example of strength through service to others, not to self.

It is important to note that these four leaders—Tutu, Mandela, King, and Gandhi—redefined the power of nonviolence in modern times. They established a kind of peace that would not be possible with traditional warfare. These recent historical examples exemplify the power of a compassionate community as opposed to the shortcomings of a dictatorship. Kingdoms based on traditional power rise and fall, but God's love is eternal.

It can be difficult to see our personal roles as Christians in today's complex and often chaotic global situation. Because of our fears, we tend to retreat inward and ignore the needs of the community. It is especially difficult to see ourselves as evangelists, spreading the good news of the Christian community. We don't have to be Peter, Paul, or the other apostles. But when we read their stories, we are reminded that, as with the first Christians, the gift of the Holy Spirit is present in today's community of believers. Acts of our own do make a difference. When we are truly in communion with Christ and experiencing the peace that passes all understanding, others come to warm up in our presence, which is the presence of Christ who is in us.

Among earnest Christians in the Church today there is a growing desire to meet together with other Christians in the rest periods of their work for common life under the Word.[7]
—Dietrich Bonhoeffer, *Life Together*

I have shared one story again and again, a story among stories about a true Christian community. Different versions of this story exist and have appeared in various publications over the years. Credit for telling it has gone to M. Scott Peck, but he admits it is not his creation. No one knows its origin, but it describes a world that could be—far beyond the world in which we now live. The story, "The Rabbi's Gift," introduces the compassionate world that Jesus teaches about and hopes for us all to discover. It is a story of the work of the Holy Spirit; not as profound a work as what happened on Pentecost when the Spirit descended on the first Christians. But all the same, the Holy Spirit is still present. There is no speaking in many languages, no tongues of fire, no profound revelation, but there is a love for the community in which the characters all have membership. And that is enough to change the world. Here is the story:

The monastery with the chapel on the hill had fallen apart; no one wished to come anymore. Just three elderly monks were left in this dilapidated old order. Once a solid chapel, now it stood in ruin, with no money to fix it and no congregation to care.

The three brothers constantly blamed each other. "No one is here because of the two of you, if you weren't so mean, people might come!" the first brother would say.

Another one said, "Your frustration caused our entire congregation to leave and not come back!"

And the third brother would say, "It is the two of you who caused us this problem, for you two think only of yourselves!"

On and on it went, month after month and year after year. The brothers remained frustrated with each other.

One day a rabbi came to visit his three friends at this dying chapel. The three brothers pleaded with the rabbi for advice to save the monastery. They dined together and cried together. Even the rabbi could tell that the Spirit had left his three friends, and he knew that the people who lived down in the village below the chapel had also lost the Spirit.

The rabbi left with these words, "I am so sorry I couldn't save the chapel, but I know the Messiah lives in one of you." And with that he left. What was this strange message that the rabbi left them? Could it be a code for something bigger? Could he possibly be talking about one of them? The brothers contemplated.

In the days that followed, the three brothers pondered the statement of the rabbi. "Maybe the Messiah lives in my brother. No, maybe it is me that he lives in. Or maybe it is in my other brother."

As they continued to ponder the statement, something miraculous began to happen. From the thought of Christ living in the heart of one of the brothers, an extraordinary respect for all of the brothers began to grow. The glow of compassion, respect, and love began to exude from each of them, and it was both attractive and contagious. The aura began to flow down the hill and into the village. Within a short time, villagers began to wander toward the old chapel to warm up in its glow. The Spirit was in the air. Before long, the chapel became a center for a thriving community once again—thanks to the rabbi's gift.

While the Spirit is important, a monastery, church, or other community starts, struggles, and grows, because of a disciplined compassion. Unless one wins the lottery or receives an inheritance, one does not become wealthy without financial discipline. A person cannot become healthy overnight either. Doing so takes a lifetime of disciplined eating and exercise. Of course, our ancestors thought very little about either fitness or finances. Certainly, they prayed for good health and enough food for their families, but for the majority of the population in the agricultural age, fitness was a given because of the intense physical activity that life demanded. And money was not readily available. A good crop was gold. Feeding the family and being able to sell the excess for a small profit was the best any farmer could ask for. Also, families stayed together for the benefit of all, not just the individual. Hard physical labor and faith are all that men and women of early America had—hard physical labor and faith that God would make it rain.

For the men and women of the agricultural age, fitness had a greater purpose—it was a matter of life and death. If the cow wasn't milked, she would dry up and the baby would have no milk. If the crops were not harvested, there would be no food. The more fit you were, the more potential you had to create food. The more fit you were, the more good you could do for your family and those neighbors who could not do for themselves.

Today, things are better, or at least less physically demanding. As a result, however, it seems that finances and fitness have become the dominant topics of self-help books, videos, and infomercials. Modern conveniences have vastly improved our quality of life. The basic things that used to take all day are done in moments and with great ease. We have moved from a culture of physical labor to one of mental labor. Instead of the nation picking crops by hand, a handful of farmers efficiently use modern machinery while the rest of us do other things to meet people's needs. And in theory, we have more free time to spend with family and friends.

However, people in America now spend less quality time with family and friends than previous generations. Robert Putnam, in his book, *Bowling Alone,* shows a detailed trend in which most all the groups, clubs, events, or routines that used to draw us together in community have declined sharply in the last fifty years. Church attendance, PTA, league bowling, social groups, political parties, and civic clubs all have decreased in membership and participation. Along with this trend toward less group interaction and participation, there had been a rise in entertainment and spectator activities such as television, sporting events, and movies along with a general increase in prosperity. As we choose "spectator" activities, we move away from the interactive contacts common to the two or three generations before us. The conclusion is that there is a sharp disconnection with each other over the last half of the twentieth century in the way we choose to spend our time.[8] In the first years of the twenty-first century, reality television, Internet downloads for entertainment, computer games, and at-home movies have sharply increased in popularity among American consumers, so it appears that the trend is continuing.

While we engage less with one another, what contacts we have seem to be more competitive. Our lifestyles drive us to overachieve in every arena. We focus on relationships for networking on what is advantageous to business, rather than on spiritual, personal, or otherwise enriching relationships. We do not seem to value being in communion with one another. While we are getting more connected via the Internet, we, as a society, are becoming less connected on the true community level.

"One body, many parts" is the language Paul uses in a letter to the church at Corinth to describe all people having different skills and interests, but working together. This "one body" refers to the true community of Christians all moving toward the common goal of genuine community. The key is that one part of the body cannot act independently and get the job done; it takes contributions from all of the parts of the body to be successful. Christ asks all of us to join him in service and communion in order for every one of us to be whole and be a true community.

The true Christian community strives for the common good of the whole body, not in competition for position among its members. *True community* is a term we will use in referring a group of individuals who relate wholly, without secrets or judgment. In his book, *The Different Drum*, author M. Scott Peck describes the necessary steps to arrive at true community. He mentions that it is practically unavoidable to move from pseudo-community to true community without first passing through chaos and emptiness.[9] Think of it this way: When you meet someone you like to be around, you start spending time together, establishing what he calls pseudo-community. Eventually, something happens to cause a difference of opinion. White lies tend to appear at this point in a relationship. But, if you choose to speak the truth, you unavoidably cause some degree of conflict (chaos). This may be followed by hurt feelings (emptiness), but a new understanding is reached based on truth. Some relationships go no further. Some people reunite as closer friends with a deeper understanding for each other, a true community. Conflicts that follow are easier to deal with. True community is without pretense. A true community of believers is how God intended us to live with each other. Love your neighbor as yourself describes a loving true community.

Most senior adults who are contented at the end of their lives desire to live in true community—a community without pretense or facades. To live in this state of mind one must achieve total honesty with oneself, to be set free. It is a life that cannot be lived in isolation.

In contrast, we have witnessed horribly isolated teens who turn against their classmates with random acts of violence. At Columbine High School in Colorado and in the series of massacres that followed, youth who were marginalized by the larger community acted out by doing the unthinkable. The boys lived in isolation; they were frustrated and in communion with no one.

As we become more involved with Internet chat rooms, television, video games, and artificial communications, we can lose a sense of community. Non-verbal communications cannot take place. A persona hidden behind a computer terminal or on a cell phone is not completely whole. A simple discipline like eye contact during conversation is lost when one is not physically in communion with the other.

I recently chaperoned a group of high school youth to a national church gathering of more than thirty thousand young people. As the week went on, the intensity of the event brought the community together in many ways. Embracing, worshiping, and affirming each other through personal conversation all became more and more a part of the intentional outcome of the event.

After a few days, I discovered that four of the male youth I was responsible for were leaving the large group interaction times to go to the makeshift computer room that was provided by the event staff in a different end of the same convention center. It was a small room with about ten or twelve computers and monitors set up in a row. The computers were connected to the Internet so that, throughout the week, participants could check e-mail if they wished. Behind the computer screens, not more than three feet away from each other, these four youth discussed amongst themselves the intensity of what was happening at the event. It was behind the computer screens that these youth were safe from being vulnerable or emotionally exposed to others. They were not the only ones. The computer room was full. Other young people from many churches sought comfort behind their "screen names" when the large group gatherings got too personal.

True community lives face-to-face, not through media technology. True community's only requirement is giving your whole self, being completely present and completely honest. Networking purely for self-interest or any other ulterior motive will stand in the way of your being "real." You must be you: imperfect, broken, and honest. In order to reach true community, one must risk pain and vulnerability, in trust and love. Otherwise, a community will always remain superficial, with walls between its members. Honest steps taken through the chaos and emptiness end in true community with a deeper respect and understanding about the others in communion—when love is the catalyst.

Each time we commune with Christ in love, we leave with a deeper understanding of his mercy and are mended from our own brokenness. We pass from our own life's chaos, become exposed and vulnerable in our own emptiness before him, and then, with his love as the catalyst, we are with Christ in true community. At the cross, we kneel as a broken community, but are together as a true community.

It is more important than ever, in our age of elevated violence and our ample weapons of mass destruction, that we strive to live in true community with love and concern for all people—especially our enemies. Jesus' command to love our enemies is more than just a nice suggestion—it is a lesson intended to save humanity.

Live in true community. Love your neighbor. Switch the price tags on the material things that we as a society have labeled as valuable with the fruits of the Spirit by embracing the community around you as Christ taught.

The treadmill of consumerism pushes us to want to earn more. In that pursuit of more, numerous hours are spent on overtime, second jobs, and women working outside the home. (In 1900, 21 percent of the workforce was women; in 1999, women became the dominate gender in the workplace at 60 percent.)[10] Things are exchanged for time. Time is our most valuable commodity, and that has created a hunger for speed. We desire everything to be available faster, completed more quickly, and accomplished more efficiently. The more we acquire, the more time we have to sacrifice away from other interests—such as true community and our own wellness. Both true community and wellness take disciplined time and effort, which is why they are often neglected.

Buddha taught that the more one has, the more one has to worry about. When Jesus called to his disciples, he said to give up everything and follow him. I used to think that he said that to test his followers to see if they were willing to do it. Now I've come to realize that he wisely did not want them to be distracted by "stuff." He wanted them to stay focused. He wanted them to have more time with him caring for others and less time caring for their stuff. Inspired and effective leadership!

In the next two sections you will hear the collective voices of thousands of senior adults who I had the privilege to care for as physical therapy patients over two decades. Before they passed away, these elderly women and men left a clear message: more is not better. In the end, the simple, loving, true Christian community and the close relationships that they had established had given meaning to their lives. A contented life had nothing to do with material possessions, power, or status. While the possessions rusted away, love remained.

So now we have discussed the cross of Christ and the Christian community. Why did we spend so much time speaking about community? That is a good question to ask. Maybe your goal for reading this book is to learn new techniques for staying healthy. Or possibly your interest is in losing weight. We will address these issues as we unpack the sections on food and exercise; but for now, just know that your own personal health can greatly affect everyone! The whole global community will be helped when you discipline yourself toward a life of true wellness.

Christ wishes for us to welcome and care for all people (Matthew 5:44, 7:12, and 10:40-42). When we do
this, we change ourselves and others for the better. The
Christian community embodies Christ's presence this
side of the cross. The community is Christ's gift.

Questions to Ponder

Who makes up your community? How do you live
as a member of one or more true communities?

Contented

"Come to me, all you that are weary and are carrying
heavy burdens, and I will give you rest."
    —Matthew 11:28

While looking out over the snow-covered ground outside of his second story window in rural eastern Pennsylvania, Walter drifts in and out of shallow catnaps.
This has been his daily routine for nearly two years,
with few breaks. There were the two Christmas events
when his son brought him out of the nursing home, and
the several day-trips he took on the community bus.
But every other day since he'd moved there included
the routine of watching the seasons change out of his
window.

From a distance he hears the faint sound of the
golden oldies station. It is Glenn Miller. Walter is awake
again and reliving the tremendous feeling of freedom
when returning home from Italy after the war ended.

Wide awake, Walter is pleased and content as he reflects on his life.

His body was different then. He has a picture of himself and a few army buddies on his wall. One soldier in the photo never came home. While sailing on two very small ships, they were ambushed by German soldiers. The rear vessel went down with no survivors. Walter was in the lead boat, and the eight men on his boat survived. In the picture, the soldiers are dressed in their green army fatigues, which look a non-distinct dark shade in the faded black-and-white picture. His posture is upright, heavily muscled, with straight legs, and shoulders that do not slump forward as they do now. He stands with perfect posture sixty years earlier.

After the war, Walter had returned to work as an accountant. His occupation required long hours of sitting. His diet during those years was ethnically laced with Pennsylvania Dutch pan fried potatoes and large portions of meat. On rare occasions he ate seasonal vegetables and fruit. He had no set exercise patterns or routines all his adult life.

Nearing ninety, Walter's physical condition includes a compression fracture of a vertebra between his shoulder blades, an old hip fracture with a total hip replacement, shoulder problems, and neck pain with prior surgery for arthritis. Arthritis has conquered the knees as well. In addition to this, Walter is unable to stand erect because of arthritis and muscle weakness. Unfortunately, this keeps him in a wheelchair. If a body is limited to a sitting position, endurance is greatly compromised. The heart, lungs, and circulation are significantly affected.

And of course, without the freedom of movement, obesity becomes a problem.

Walter's legs are contracted. Because of being in a constant sitting position for more than two years, he is unable to stand or extend his knees completely straight. His loss of flexibility causes pain in his back and legs when he attempts to stand.

When an adult body does not get exercised, it will lose its strength and muscle mass. This is a natural process. A human can lose up to 1 percent of his or her muscle size every year after the age of twenty-five. This natural process is called sarcopenia (sarco-muscle, penia-loss). It is easy to see how this can begin to lead to an early disability by robbing the leg muscles of the strength to carry the weight of the body or even lift it from a chair.

Let's look at Walter's shoulders. He has what is called a rotator cuff tear. Unfortunately, he has it in both shoulders. The rotator cuff is four small muscles that hold the shoulder joint in place while the big muscles of the shoulder move the arm. The muscles of the rotator cuff are thin to begin with and, as we age, due to the effects of sarcopenia, they get thinner and weaker. One day, when a senior citizen reaches for something heavy or catches himself from a fall, the rotator cuff tears. Unfortunately, with a tear, the arm does not work well. Reaching overhead becomes nearly impossible. Lifting heavy objects also becomes very difficult. Even though it is a small group of muscles, they can cause a great deal of disability. Surgery and a lengthy rehabilitation can correct the problem a great majority of the time. More than four million Americans seek surgeons for shoulder problems of this type each year.

In Walter's case, his spinal and hip fractures were a direct result of osteoporosis. Osteoporosis is loss of bone mineral in which the remainder of the bone is brittle and easily fractured. Commonly, hip and compression fractures of the vertebrae occur due to the loss of bone mass. Posture changes in older adults are usually caused by the combined effects of osteoporosis, sarcopenia, and gravity. Endurance declines with lack of exercise and the body becomes quickly disabled—unable to move a distance without becoming short of breath. Obesity becomes a factor when activity is diminished. Flexibility is lost when a muscle or joint is not used or exercised through its normal available range of motion.

So Walter sits, remembering the days of youth when he did not need a wheelchair. He subconsciously sees a wartime event that plays over and over in his head. It is a time when he and another army private found two German soldiers. The mission was to walk them at gunpoint many miles to where the base was so they could be kept as prisoners. Evening was coming and the sky was darkening. Walter insisted that they carry through the mission, while the other private, in fear for his life, felt they needed to dispose of the prisoners.

After walking several more miles along a river, evening came and the paranoia increased for both of these American heroes. The men were forced to be guided by only the sound of the rushing water, because sight was no longer useful. Without further consultation, Walter's companion knelt the two prisoners next to the river and shot both of them, each with a single bullet in the back of their heads. Years later, Walter would say through misty eyes, "It was wartime. That private wasn't thinking rationally like he would at other times."

This scenario replayed in Walter's head many times since 1944. When I first saw him staring out the window, I would think, "What can he possibly be thinking about?" But once I got to know him, I understood that Walter was searching for ways that he could have intervened to save the lives of the two German human beings. For you see, Walter is a contented elderly man. He is gentle and compassionate. He says his prayers not just at night, but many times through the day. He is a real treat for the nursing home staff. Oftentimes, he is chosen by the employees of the home as someone to celebrate. Administrators like to introduce him to potential residents' families because of his pleasant demeanor and the sincere, playful banter that he is able to engage others in. Walter is contented. He has a strong sense of self and purpose. Unfortunately, someone did not let him know thirty years ago that if he were to exercise and balance his diet better, he probably would not need the wheelchair now and most likely would be functional and ambulatory at one hundred years old.

The good news is that the effects of sarcopenia (muscle loss) can be reversed. It is done with exercise, specifically resistance exercise. Resistance exercise involves weights, bands, or weight machines.

Osteoporosis responds positively to resistance exercises as well. In fact, healthcare professionals suggest resistance exercises and weight-bearing exercises, such as walking or jogging, to stimulate stronger bones to fight the effects of aging and osteoporosis.

Posture, endurance, and flexibility can all be affected positively with the right exercises. The heart, lungs, and circulation become more efficient. Flexibility is maintained. As activity increases and muscles grow larger from resistance exercises, calories burn more efficiently. Thus, obesity is reversed. And, of course, proper diet affects all of the above for the better.

At this stage of Walter's life, to walk again, to stand up straight, and to have his fragile body keep up with his nimble mind would be wonderful. Walter is thankful for his nimble mind. In fact, he is thankful for many things. His grateful attitude is a significant part of what makes him contented and loving toward others. It is why family, friends, and nursing home employees visit him daily. Even with his frailties and painful memories, he allows love for others to direct his conduct. In fact, the elder adults who understand the power of love are the ones who are most likely to be contented with their lives at this stage. They are the ones who receive the majority of the voluntary visitors at the nursing homes. It is the love they possess that overshadows the discomfort of memories past and the pain of feeble bodies—bodies that were once sturdy and capable.

Reflecting on what is important throughout the marathon of life, most senior adults agree that love is the ultimate prize and the reason to keep running. It may not always be clear during the race, but it is crystal clear at the finish.

What is love? Defining love only limits its significance. Love is pure. In a sense, to love something is to understand and respect its significance. It is the great equalizer. Paul, the great evangelist who authored much of the New Testament, says in the letter to the Corinthians that you can have absolutely everything in the world, but without love, you are a noisy gong. Love is all these things: patient, kind, humble, and generous. Love protects; it trusts and it hopes. Love is not greedy, boastful, demanding, apathetic, or uncaring. It does not keep a record of wrongs or delight in evil, but rejoices in the truth.

M. Scott Peck offers a solid definition of love for this text in his book *The Road Less Traveled*. It reads, "Love: The will to extend one's self for the purpose of nurturing one's own or another's spiritual growth."[11] In other words, it is to freely give of yourself for the benefit of helping yourself grow. Likewise, loving another is to give of yourself for the benefit of someone else's growth. To love yourself, you must understand and respect your own significance. In order to love another person, you must do the same for him or her.

This understanding and respect of others equips a nurse and colleague, Mary Jane, to care for profoundly mentally and physically challenged adults in a Pennsylvania state institution. For more than thirty years she has gone to work maintaining that she is in a position of honor because she is allowed to work every day with "God's pure souls."

This same understanding of and respect for others led Mother Teresa to work with the orphans of India. As she was working with severely needy children, a reporter told Mother Teresa, "I wouldn't do what you are doing for a million dollars," who simply but profoundly replied, "Neither would I."[12] Truly it is only love that can beget this kind of commitment to others.

In order to love others, you need to extend yourself to others. Extending is an action. Unlike romantic love or "falling in love," real love is not passive. Real love requires disciplined action. Real love requires discipline of yourself and ongoing commitment to others.

On the cross, Christ extended himself to others unto death. We are called to take up our own cross and follow the leader into action, proclaiming the good news. Through the Scriptures, Christ reveals to us that our time is best spent showing compassion, loving unconditionally, feeding his sheep, and proclaiming his gospel message. In so doing, we affirm our belief in Christ—which gives our lives meaning.

We have been given a window looking into our own futures. So many senior adults embrace love as a primary motive in life. Again and again, stories echo the significance of a fulfilled life when love is the catalyst. During their final years, many seniors feel a life of fulfillment with love. Sadly, those who lived a self-serving existence reflect something very different in their final years. Either way, we can learn from what they have to teach us.

Questions to Ponder

What have been the most contented periods
of your life, and who were the people who
made up your community during those times?
Why do you suppose love was so easy
to feel during those contented times?

Frustrated

> To set the mind on the flesh is death, but to set the
> mind on the Spirit is life and peace.
>   —Romans 8:6

Charles Dickens immortalized the character of Ebenezer
Scrooge. The outlook of this character changed overnight with the help of three ghosts. The story ends with
Ebenezer understanding the value of loving your neighbor. That story speaks to us so plainly because it plays
out the consequences of our free choice to be in communion with or in competition with the community around
us. Unfortunately, in real life we don't get the help of
three well-meaning ghosts. We are given free choice to
make that decision for ourselves about how we see our
community. Sometimes we make the wrong choice.

Mary was frustrated. She was in her late seventies,
focused on her own needs, and incensed at the fact that
her disabilities kept her from her activities. Mary had a
niece who helped her with daily activities, but she had
no husband or children. The niece visited her out of family obligation. Mary had a sister, but they were not close.
She had no real relationships and no friends. Everyone
avoided her—except out of duty. She was intolerant of
the staff. Mary had no other visitors.

But her roommate had visitors and, during one of
those visits, a curtain opened. On the other side of the
curtain was a cute six-year-old girl who was spending
time with her grandma in the next bed. Mary pointed
to the girl and said, "Put me in another room. I hate
kids, and I don't want anything to do with them." The

family visiting will never forget those words, especially the little girl. It was obvious to see that anyone entering Mary's life was soon destroyed in the wake of her massive frustration and anger. She affected everyone by her mere presence. As a highly educated former athlete, she had all the advantages growing up. But she appeared to be incapable of love or even establishing a lasting friendship. Her life was isolated, and she lived in a self-serving manner. This preoccupation with herself intensified as she grew older. She had a nimble mind, but chose to focus on her feeble body and forgo giving thanks for what she did have.

Like Walter, Mary had shoulder, knee, hip, and neck problems. She was affected by osteoporosis, sarcopenia, and postural difficulties. She had problems with obesity and, as with Walter, the effects of the ailments could have been reduced or reversed if Mary had disciplined herself with proper exercise and healthy habits.

Unfortunately, Mary was unable to find peace. There was no love in her life. She experienced severe depression and harbored resentment toward all others who did not have her disabilities. Even if her physical problems had been cured, Mary would have drawn the same conclusion about life—it had no purpose.

"Blessed are the pure in heart, for they will see God" (Matthew 5:8). Once this is understood, once a life is lived with a pure heart—full of mercy and compassion and not just concern for its own existence—life becomes meaningful. Those seniors who have lived lives of only self-concern come to the end of life with an increased tendency toward frustration and depression. Faith, true faith, reduces stress, lengthens life, and counters depression.

Dr. Harold G. Koenig, while serving as director of Duke University's Center for the Study of Religion/Spirituality and Health, determined the following: "People with strong religious faith are less likely to suffer depression from stressful life events, and if they do, they are more likely to recover from depression than those who are less religious."[13]

The value of exercise as a counter to depression has been proven again and again. Much as addictive substances such as alcohol, cocaine, and tobacco stimulate the areas of the brain that cause cravings for more; so does exercise. Routine exercise has been found to affect the same neurotransmitters as addictive drugs.[14] This causes a craving for ongoing exercise once exercise becomes routine.

Exercise stimulates endorphins, which function like anti-depressants. So the more you exercise, the more you desire to exercise and the less depressed you feel. Even for those individuals with Major Depressive Disorder (MDD), a single bout of exercise was found to be useful in mood regulation.[15] People who take the time to include a routine of daily exercise in their lives experience not only the physical benefits of improved strength, endurance, flexibility, balance, and a reduced risk of osteoporosis and sarcopenia, but they also experience reduced levels of depression.

> Just as junk food and lack of exercise can ruin an athlete's condition, those things that are obscene, crude, or pornographic can breed an inner darkness that numbs our higher sensibilities and substitutes the social conscience of "Will I be found out?" for the natural or divine conscience of "What is right and wrong?"[16]
> –Stephen Covey

Betty was contented, and Bob was frustrated. Betty was a former schoolteacher. She had significant arthritis and as a result had a very hard time walking more than short distances. Before she died, she spoke of how so many problems can be solved if we could just be tolerant as a nation. She had a generous, liberal view of politics and a gifted intelligence related to social matters and current events. She was able to disagree tactfully, using a gentle nudge of persuasion. Never did she utter a derogatory word. When a political debate would arise, she could soften the mood with her tone.

Bob was another senior I worked with during the year I worked with Betty. He could not tolerate Betty defending those "freeloaders" he felt did not deserve taxpayer money. He spoke often of wasted government money, while Betty spoke of the successes of welfare and school programs. Eventually, Bob could no longer be around Betty simply because he could not deal with their differences. Bob was divorced. His children did not talk or visit with him. He would say, "Those kids are just waiting for their inheritance." Bob was calloused, proud, and full of complaints. Betty was loving, contented, and full of life. Both seniors had sharp minds and were crippled with the physical effects of old age. I was there as both seniors concluded final chapters of lives: one with a happy ending, one with a sad one. "You reap whatever you sow" (Galatians 6:7).

It is a great irony that those who complain the loudest, the elderly who are the most demanding of their caretakers, are the ones who are served last. It has been my experience that the majority of nurses and nursing assistants feel they would rather care for five contented elderly clients who affirm their efforts, than the one frustrated elderly client who berates and belittles them. I would have to agree with them. A kind act of service recognized by the recipient is motivation enough to continue. For this reason, the elderly who are contented and loving receive the most visitors, the extras from the staff, and the highest quality care that can possibly be given. The frustrated elderly are likely to receive what is required and nothing more.

Caretakers are human. When a caretaker is acknowledged as a valuable member of the senior's community, caretakers become empowered to act for the person who cannot live without the help they give. Those who spend a lifetime "sowing" love for others, encouraging their spiritual growth, and helping them in service, will reap a harvest that is bountiful at the end. The final chapter becomes a pure joy and a reflection of the contented life that was lived. But when a life is spent in a self-indulgent manner, no matter what the monetary gain, the harvest in the end is pitifully scarce. The frustrated ones are cared for minimally and only out of obligation, not out of genuine love.

> This is the true joy in life—that being used for a purpose recognized by yourself as a mighty one. That being a force of nature, instead of a feverish, selfish little clod of ailments and grievances complaining that the world will not devote itself to making you happy. I am of the opinion that my life belongs to the whole community and as long as I live it is my privilege to do for it whatever I can. I want to be thoroughly used up when I die. For the harder I work

the more I live. I rejoice in life for its own sake. Life is no brief candle to me. It's a sort of splendid torch which I've got to hold up for the moment and I want to make it burn as brightly as possible before handing it on to future generations.[17]
   —George Bernard Shaw

Questions to Ponder

What were the most frustrated periods of your life, and who were the people who made up your community during those times? Why do you suppose love was so hard to feel during those frustrated times?

Faith

For I am not ashamed of the gospel; it is the power of God for salvation to everyone who has faith, to the Jew first and also to the Greek. For in it the righteousness of God is revealed through faith for faith; as it is written, "The one who is righteous will live by faith."
   —Romans 1:16-17

Eula's funeral was a reflection of how she lived her life. As I climbed the steps of the pulpit to speak on the family's behalf, I looked out over the sea of friends and family who in one way or another had been touched by this ninety-seven-year-old woman. The old country church was full. It hadn't been this full since Easter Sunday service over nine months earlier. How could a lady of almost a century create such a following?

I remembered just a year before when I went to church with Eula and my three-year-old daughter. The pastor was talking about the resurrection, and my daughter was watching Eula. The two were sharing a moment—a human moment. A toy meant for a three year old was the magnet that brought these two together. Ninety-three years between them, both smiling and laughing as if there were nothing going on around them. It was that moment that made me remember what the magic was that attracted everyone to this contented senior. The sermon had been at the front of the church, but the gospel lesson was being played out right next to me. Love one another. It's as easy as that. Her life was lived, with both discipline and enthusiasm, to experience Christ through everyone, young and old, who crossed her path. Her community was vast. The hundreds of people present felt that same connection to her that my young daughter and I did. The large community of folks attending the funeral was a tribute to how she lived her life, with compassion and love. I learned more about Eula by talking to several different people at the funeral—people from all different stages of her life. Some had known her in her younger days, some were nurses who cared for her in the nursing home in Pennsylvania where she lived during her last year of life. All gave her the same endorsement by saying, "She loved everyone." It is no wonder that the church was full.

Reflecting on what is important throughout the marathon of life, most senior adults agree that love is the ultimate prize and the reason to keep running. It may not always be clear during the race, but it is crystal clear at the finish.

Viktor Frankl, author of *Man's Search for Meaning,* while in his third year of abuse and torture as a prisoner of a Nazi concentration camp, wrote, ". . . love is the ultimate and the highest goal to which man can aspire."[18]

In order to know love, one must recognize its opposites: hate, apathy, and evil. Faith in Christ assures us of God's love, even in the midst of great calamity. Faith gives us comfort that he is suffering with us, and evil does not have the last word. With faith in Christ, evil never does.

Like Viktor Frankl and Walter, many other seniors talked about their experiences of such atrocities. In almost every case, the unspeakable evil drove them toward the fundamental truth: love is the ultimate and highest goal to which we can aspire.

I first met Richard in 1993. Richard was a European immigrant, a senior citizen who came to see me every week for about six months. Richard was a great guy. The stories that he shared were not unlike many of the holocaust survivors' stories I had the privilege of hearing from other seniors who had lived through such horrors. As a young child, Richard was sent to a concentration camp where his parents were killed. His father was driven mad because he was forced to watch the Nazis skin fellow prisoners. Yet, Richard was contented and a pleasure to work with over fifty years after his extremely tragic experience.

When you are in your twenties and you are severely injured, it's hard to imagine how you will be coping with your disability sixty years later. Arnold was on the front lines with the Latvian army in WWII, fighting the Russians, when he lost his leg. Sixty years later, he and his wife were among the most contented and loving seniors I have known. Arnold's wife would say, "You forget the bad, and the good things stay with you." Then she would add, "Our faith in God and better days to come got us through."

Bill was another veteran injured in battle, and he also lost many men during the twenty-three years he served in the U.S. Navy. He shared his stories as he taught me how to grow tomatoes to perfection.

Don lost his son to diabetes. Still, he talked about how he could get lost in nature by fly-fishing at his home in Wisconsin. He would become one with nature for hours at a time, and reach a peace that he imagined heaven being like. Don told me once, "You need to fill your head with beautiful memories because when you are really old and sitting there, you'll have nothing but those memories. I don't want to say, 'I should have, I could have . . .'" Don is contented and loving. He cherishes the time he had with his son.

I'll never forget Anna. Anna was seventy-five when she shared with me how she was exiled from Yugoslavia into Germany at seventeen years old in 1944. She was forced to make ammunition for the Germans to fight against the Allied forces. Her brother and father were fighting for the Allied forces. With every bullet she made she wondered if this would be the one that killed the most important people in her life. Anna learned to cope. It is truly amazing to me how these individuals over the years kept their faith in God and humanity.

Love has faithfully given these contented seniors a solid motivation and purpose in life. It is their common love that renews them, replenishes them, and gives them comfort. Love reduces their emotional pain. Love is their safety net, God's shoulder to lean on. Without love, these seniors would be forced to contemplate all of life's difficulties alone. Without love, life's highs are dampened or less meaningful. Their faith in a loving God, even with the atrocities they experienced, made them whole. As Christians, the suffering we experience in life doesn't go away, it is shared—with Jesus and the rest of the community.

If, as stated by Viktor Frankl, "love is the ultimate and the highest goal to which man can aspire," our personal wellness depends on each of us accepting the truth that God loves us. God chooses to do it; Jesus made this clear on the cross. By God's grace alone and not our own doing, we are deemed worthy to die for. This is how we know how deeply we are loved. All other aspects of our lives depend on this understanding. Our belief in a loving God leads us to further believe God has provided for us and wishes for us to share in community—not serve only our own self-interest. God wants to nurture our spiritual growth.

When a child touches a hot stove, pain is felt and the child, in his limited knowledge, labels heat as bad or evil. Only through further observation and experience does he realize that heat provides warmth and comfort in the cold, and hot water for cleaning and cooking food. Eventually, the child learns that heat brings life. The old paradigm or belief that heat is evil is dropped in favor of the new understanding that heat is good and necessary.

A child has a painful experience, interprets the incident as best she can, and builds a belief around that experience. She might even experience God as evil or indifferent toward her because of a situation that happens. The child concludes, "I must have deserved what I got because God did not come to my rescue in my time of need" or "God just doesn't love me." It is this kind of experience, without others to modify it, which keeps some adult children from growing spiritually. They stay wounded.

Like the old understanding of heat, the old, limited belief of the love of God may take new insights to correct. The Christian community can provide such positive life experiences and new insights to the wounded.

God loves us! Without believing this, we cannot understand the harmony of our co-existence with nature, with ourselves, and with each other. If one comes to believe in God's loving nature through Christ, one can begin to grasp God's provisions for us through food and exercise.

For the affluent, this much is certain: there will always be plenty of new diets, appetite suppressants, medicines, and fitness devices to fight the battle of overabundance. Although these items can be helpful, weight-loss attempts not understood beyond our own self-interests, traditionally fail in due time. Old habits override the best intentions of any individual. But, our issue of overabundance is only half of the global problem. Understanding the scarce resources of our brothers and sisters who have nothing will complete our global picture and enrich our perspective.

It took a long time to arrive where we are now in this thinking. We spent time with the cross of Christ and his community. We discussed the futility of material pursuits, the physical breakdown of the aging body, and the faith stories of older adults. Now, and only now, are we ready to talk about a lifetime of wellness through healthy eating and exercising.

From here on, weight loss and fitness will not be explored as goals in themselves, motivated by the scale and the mirror. We will investigate how they can add to the length and depth of our lives, to our love for our neighbors, and our love for God. Thank you for being patient. Wellness now has a much greater goal. The goal is not fleeting or temporary; it is for life. Our health is not just for us, but for others as well. The entire global community benefits from our food choices and our healthy habits.

Remember these two key points: First, God created the world in a way that gives us all the provisions and nutrition a person needs for a healthy and full life. Second, unlike everything made by humans, the body rebuilds, strengthens, and improves with consistent use, and weakens when not used appropriately.

Questions to Ponder

What aspects of your faith connect you with believers around the world and throughout time? How does one person's faith in a loving and merciful God, as revealed in Jesus, benefit the global community?

Chapter 2: Food

We search for more answers because the ones we have
found are not to our liking.
  —Joel Fuhrman, M.D. *Eat to Live*[1]

Food for Thought

So, whether you eat or drink, or whatever you do, do
everything for the glory of God.
  —1 Corinthians 10:31

An interesting change has taken place in the food industry since World War I. From the humble beginnings of simple agriculture—before fortifying and enriching, mass farming, pesticides, insecticides, commercial canning, frozen and fast foods—the food industry has evolved into the giant it is today. Over the years, the food we eat has changed drastically. Food is now globally prepackaged and processed, whereas for the six to ten thousand years before, it was eaten directly after harvesting, raw, or possibly cooked. As early as 1939, it was said that Mother Nature "included all the necessary vitamins in basic raw food materials" and "modern food processing and preserving methods impaired the potency of these vitamins".[2] But, people continued to buy processed foods with additives instead of fresh foods. It was also understood early that those advocating food fads, like new diet products, are more successful in gaining acceptance of their ideas than are the professional nutritionists.[3] As early as 1959, *Time* magazine stated "that the emphasis in the food business has moved more and more from manufacturing to marketing.[4]

Alice, a contented elder, was a product of the great depression, as were most of the people born before the 1930s. She remembered the struggles her parents went through in order to provide food for all the children. She would say, "You just did what you had to do, there was not a choice, no handouts, and everyone scrambled to support each other." Hunger was a painful truth. Even in her eighties, Alice could not imagine wasting food. She couldn't imagine taking more than her share knowing someone else might be in need.

The food industry is a huge business today. As of 2002, if we include all aspects from the soil to the dinner table, the food industry is 13 percent of the Gross National Product, or a trillion dollars.[5] It includes everything from fertilizers to grocery stores. In fact, the total of those involved with the food industry in the United States is about 17 percent of the labor force.[6] In America, we produce enough food to give approximately 3,800 calories daily to each American.[7] This is nearly twice the amount that is required or recommended by the United States Deptartment of Agriculture (USDA) for individuals.

A startling and paradoxical truth that we face is that we spend considerably more and more each year on diets (in the billions),[8] yet the obesity rate among Americans continues to rise each year. We have a surplus of food within our grasp. Food companies all compete for our attention by making their products more appealing to our tastes. Meanwhile, more than a billion people worldwide don't know where their next meal will come from. Even with this awareness, obesity continues to escalate in America and in other wealthy nations.

Our trillion-dollar food industry tells us to eat more. Our doctors say eat less. We wish we could control ourselves and not eat so much, especially while poor people, our brothers and sisters, have no food to eat. Is something terribly wrong with the fundamentals of our current scenario? Do you feel heartbroken about the imbalance? If you do, that is good. Compassionate action can only come about with a changed heart. Hang in there. You can be a vessel God uses for the fundamental switch that will begin to right the wrong. You can be an advocate for the poor, while you balance your own personal health issues. Your awakening to this great injustice can spark others, and they may awaken others. America can see the light—lose weight, get healthy, and feed the poor. This can happen, not just in theory, but in action—through compassion and through the local church.

The diet industry continues to strive for new products and new cure-alls for weight loss. As early as 1960, $500 million was spent on food fads, extreme diets, and cure-alls.[9] Because weight loss tends to be an emotional issue, the products sell well, even if they are not thoroughly researched. Many times, if a cure for weight loss is advertised, it will sell even if found unsafe. A weight-loss product in the 1990s was a top seller even though it was linked to eight hundred side effects and at least twenty deaths.[10] In spite of these warnings, the sales were still in the millions. Unfortunately, this was not a one-time case. Weight-loss products continue to sell, whatever warnings they carry. New products in different forms and packages are all advertised to be the only shortcut to wellness and permanent slimness. The nation continues to pay billions on false hope.

We fight having an abundance of food, while outside our land of milk and honey our neighbors starve. In a world of plenty, a fifth of the planet's people are so poor, their very survival is in doubt. In fact, eight million people around the world die each year because they are too poor to stay alive.[11] But starvation is a food distribution problem.

In the first chapter, we talked about a paradigm shift or change in belief taught by contented senior adults. This change in belief simplifies our lives and allows love, not money (or any *thing* else) to be the primary motivator for our actions. In the end, love is what makes a life that was worth living. If a second shift were to happen, from the current need-to-lose-weight paradigm to a need-to-feed-others paradigm, this nation would lose weight more easily. More importantly, we would feed the poor, as Christ commanded. Ultimately, these two shifts in our thinking are parallel and motivate us not to focus on our own weight or health problems, but on the needs of our global community. By broadening our mission from our personal weight issues to the health of the global community, we demonstrate compassionate wellness, and our personal weight issues become significantly less challenging. The switch from struggling with our own abundance to addressing the needs of our neighbors will awaken our deeper hunger that is not satisfied with food: the need to truly love our neighbor.

That which is true, right, or good awakens in us a deeper understanding of purpose. Acting on behalf of our neighbors in the Third World is a major step toward this monumental shift of thinking. When someone with abundance is emotionally and spiritually connected to the millions with little or no food, he or she becomes acutely aware of the injustice of the imbalance of food distribution in the world. Without the experience of seeing it firsthand, one's biggest food decisions might include deciding which restaurant to go to or whether to eat a second or third helping at the all-you-can-eat buffet! With a paradigm shift, the appetite for excess is lost. Overeating causes guilt, not because one might gain weight, but because of the deep compassion for those who have nothing. It is hard to overeat when remembering the face of a person who goes without food, a person whose only crime is to be born in an unfortunate place.

We have been very well trained on food do's and don'ts. But focusing on food control still keeps one's mind on food and not on the bigger picture. When we show compassion for the poor, we take a bold step back to refocus. And then, by eating only our share and feeding the poor with our abundance, we "feed" the healthy and moral way of thinking. Rabbi Harold Kushner tells of a Native American Indian tribal leader who describes his daily struggle of right and wrong as two dogs that fight for position. One dog is right (truth, good) and the other is wrong (untruth, bad). When a listener asks which dog usually wins, he responds, "The one I feed the most."[12] Feed what is good and right to feed.

Self-awareness through occasional fasting also creates the deeper understanding of those who go without.

Hunger pangs remind us vividly and concretely of those who have nothing. Fasting enhances our appreciation of the food we do have as well. The individual can end a fast by simply going to the cupboard or refrigerator. Those who are impoverished do not have that luxury. The prayers of fasting individuals are deeper and more appreciative of the food they are about to receive. After fasting, one treats food differently, with a new respect.

Starting to understand the difference between food wants and true hunger awakens a deeper hunger—a hunger for truth. It is this deeper hunger that is only achieved by exposing that which shadows the truth. The greater hunger is satisfied when one connects to the needs of those less fortunate and sees clearly for the first time. Never again will one complain about food overabundance with a full mouth. Never again will one feel that food overabundance is a curse.

> If we are touched by the images of men, women, and children that we have seen starving for food, it is because they are a reflection of our own need. They are a reminder not only of that part of us that is hungry, but also of that part of us that needs to give in order to be whole.[13]

Questions to Ponder
How do you respond to the guilt of your overabundance? What images make you feel too guilty to overeat?

Real Food

An intriguing twenty-five-year study of the longest-living people in the world suggests that diet, exercise, faith practices, and personal relationships are the reasons for their longevity. The people of Okinawa, located off the coast of Japan, have the lowest occurrence of heart disease in the world—one-fifth that of the United States. Occurrence of breast, ovarian, and prostate cancer is significantly lower than that of the United States too. There are six times as many one-hundred-year-old people per capita there as in America. The world's longest disability-free life expectancies are also in Okinawa.[14]

The people of Okinawa have a strong sense of community, with high levels of social contact. Prayers are often about health. Health and longevity are celebrated, and the elderly are respected and considered wise. There are also extremely low levels of negative emotions and depression.

In Okinawa, the diet of the islanders is vegetables (especially leafy greens), 34 percent; whole grains, 32 percent; lean proteins (fish), 11 percent; soy, 12 percent; fruit, 6 percent; and meat/eggs/poultry/seaweed, 5 percent.[15] That means that almost 70 percent of the diet of the healthiest humans in the world consists of vegetables and whole grains.

The November 2005 issue of *National Geographic* tells the stories of three communities of elderly who reside in completely different parts of the world. The community of Sardinia, Italy, has things in common with the communities of Okinawa, as well as the Seventh Day Adventist community of Loma Linda, California. All three have a proportionately higher number of people one hundred years old or older compared to the rest of the world.[16] What do these three communities have in common? All three have the following similarities: no smoking, family as first priority, active physical lifestyle, socially engaging communities, and healthy diets. Even though the three communities represent different regions and religions, all of them have diets that are dominated by fruits, vegetables, and whole grains.

Sardinians shepherd, Okinawans farm and fish, and the Seventh Day Adventists of Loma Linda (the healthiest Americans) serve in various positions throughout the city. All are very active, eat healthy, and have a strong sense of community and religion.

A sad truth about each community is that some threads of traditions are being broken among the generations. The taste for fast food, the use of automobiles instead of walking or bicycling, using television and other electronic media are slowly becoming the preferred alternatives to the traditional, especially for the younger generations.

Diets are among the most explored and exploited topics in recent decades. It is reasonable to say that you could find a rationale to support any diet that you like; high carbohydrates, low carbohydrates and high protein, low fat, calorie counting—diets that target blood type, vegetarian diets, and starvation diets. Some diets require supplements, powders, or specific food combinations; others are a matter of strict food control with no required supplementation.

Calorie intake is essential for life. We use calories from our diets throughout a normal day. Tampering too much, one way or the other, with caloric intake disrupts the body's natural need to stay in balance. Every day the body needs a certain number of calories, depending on one's size and activity level. When a large number of calories is taken away from a balanced diet, the body has an increased risk of losing muscle mass (or size). A smaller reduction of calories from a balanced diet with increased activity tends to make a more lasting body-fat loss.

Starting as a war effort in May of 1941, the idea of Recommended Daily Allowances (RDA) for nutrients was introduced at the National Nutrition Conference to be a yardstick for identifying a standard of nutrition. People who did not take in those recommended allowances were identified as undernourished.[17] Gradually, "undernourishment" became a national focus. As a result, processed foods, such as white bread, became "fortified" or enriched with vitamins and minerals, and the food supplement industry exploded. Since then, RDAs have been revised and updated continuously. Look at the nutrition label on any bottle, can, or package of food you buy. The United States Food and Drug Administration (USDA) developed a comprehensive standard in nutritional values. "Daily Values" (DV) are currently based on a 2,000-calorie diet, although this is always being updated as new discoveries unfold in research. The total calories and the percentages recommended for fats, proteins, and carbohydrates are part of the nutrition label. Also included are sodium, fiber, vitamins, and minerals. This system is designed for nutritional needs of average healthy adults, and is easily referred to on every container in stores. However, the system is not intended to tell individuals exactly what they need to eat each day. Let's look a little more closely at each nutrient. Again, all values are subject to change depending on the latest research, but for now, these are the standards.

Proteins: The FDA recommends that 50 grams of protein be eaten on a daily basis in a 2,000-calorie diet. These values change in proportion to the overall calories. For example, in a 1,500-calorie diet, you would only need 75 percent of the recommended 50 grams (or 37.5 grams). To better understand what 50 grams of protein is, one handful of peanuts (or 1/4 cup) is about seven grams, while two ounces of tuna fish is 14 grams. It doesn't take much to get to 50 grams in a day, if you eat healthy foods that are rich in protein. Heavy weight lifting activity and a body with a larger muscle mass increases one's need for protein. Lean (low-fat) proteins are found in almost all seafood, poultry, beans, and dark green vegetables. Nuts and seeds also have high concentrations of proteins, but with higher fat and calorie content.

Carbohydrates: The FDA recommends that up to 300 grams of carbohydrates be consumed in a 2,000-calorie a day diet. Again, in a 1,500-calorie diet, you would need 225 grams. A large whole-wheat bagel is 55 grams of carbohydrates, while eight ounces of regular orange juice has 26 grams. It is obvious that these numbers add up fast, especially with a diet of heavily processed fast foods and prepackaged food products.

Carbohydrates can raise blood sugar levels immediately by converting quickly to glucose and entering the bloodstream. When the blood sugar (glucose) level rises, so does the release of insulin from the pancreas. The more insulin released in one's system due to the intake of carbohydrates, the less stored body fat will be used for energy. Diabetes is the condition of the pancreas not being able to produce enough insulin, or any at all. Excessive insulin in the blood can block the burning of fat for energy, making it more difficult to lose body fat with exercise.

Not all carbohydrates are created equal. Much of the carbohydrates found in vegetables, fruits, and whole grains is dietary fiber. Dietary fiber is the part of the plant that cannot be digested. Even though dietary fiber is a carbohydrate, it does not cause a rise in blood sugar or a release of insulin. The FDA recommends at least 25 grams of fiber daily in a 2,000-calorie diet. Refined sugars and processed flours are the carbohydrates of the plants, fruits, and grains with the fiber removed. This process of refining leaves only the portion of carbohydrates that causes insulin to be released.

The Glycemic Index has become a very popular dietary tool with the help of diets such as the Atkins Diet®, the Zone Diet, the South Beach Diet®, SugarBusters®, Nutri-System®, and many others. This index can help determine the effect that a certain food has on the blood and the food's effect on the release of insulin. Each particular food is compared to glucose, or white bread, which has an assigned value of 100.[18] All foods with carbohydrates will affect insulin level. The Glycemic Index value of foods can be used to compare foods such as fruits and vegetables in their natural state to those that have been processed. The bottom line is, the more whole the food (the less it is processed), the lower the Glycemic Index number, which means the healthier it is for digestion and the slower release of insulin. This is primarily due to the dietary fiber content that remains in the food. Whole foods ensure the healthy fiber that was intended for a balanced diet. Fiber regulates the function of the digestive system, curbs hunger, and helps in the elimination of bacteria and cholesterol in the intestines. This is accomplished without added digested calories, increase of blood sugars, or a release of insulin. Whole foods, and especially their fiber, offer health benefits without added calories.

To put it another way, if one were to drink apple juice, almost 100 percent of the carbohydrates of that juice are carbohydrates that cause a rush of insulin to the bloodstream, thus blocking the body's ability to use stored fat for energy. If one ate the same serving as applesauce, 89 percent of the carbohydrates would affect insulin, 11 percent would not. With a whole apple, 82 percent of overall carbohydrates would affect insulin, 18 percent would not. This 18 percent is different types of healthy fiber, which aid in digestion while not adding digested calories to the overall daily caloric intake. Eating a real apple greatly reduces the assigned Glycemic Index number, putting less strain on the pancreas to release large volumes of insulin into the blood at one time. The healthiest way to eat the apple is directly from the tree. Carbohydrates from strained orange juice affect insulin 100 percent. A whole orange is 79 percent carbohydrates affecting insulin and nearly 21 percent being healthy types of fiber. The same is true for wheat. Most white bread has about 5 percent fiber, while wheat bread has 10 percent fiber. This significantly decreases the release of insulin released from the pancreas, as well as reduces the Glycemic Index number. The less processed the natural food, the better (or lower) the Glycemic Index number.

So, the Glycemic Index can be a valuable tool for determining which foods to eat in order to ensure healthy, slower, and lower release of insulin. But the simple rule of thumb is: the more real, whole, and less processed the food, with few exceptions, the healthier it is. This is the way it has been for thousands of years and still is today.

Fats: Some fat is necessary for keeping tissues in good repair, for manufacturing many hormones, and also for transporting some fat-soluble vitamins. The RDA for total fat is less than 65 grams (based on a 2,000-calorie diet). The most useful fats are found in fish and poly-unsaturated oils from plants, such as olive, canola, and flaxseed oils.

Even though some fats are useful and they do not affect the blood sugars causing the release of insulin, they are not completely out of the woods. Fats are always high in calories and don't add a tremendous amount of nutrition beyond the small amount that you can get from one or two tablespoons of cod liver oil, five ounces of walnuts, or an avocado each day. Remember, to lose body fat, you not only have to be aware of the release of insulin from carbohydrates (as many popular diets advocate), but more importantly, you need to be aware of total calories. Fatty foods can add empty calories fast.

"Good" fats can be found in real foods, such as fish and nuts. "Bad" fats are the saturated fats found in butter, meats, and dairy products. Even worse are the fats that we have created ourselves. These are found in margarine and many other processed foods, such as potato chips and doughnuts. These are the trans-fatty acids.

Vitamins and minerals: With few exceptions, all essential vitamins and minerals are found in whole grains, nuts, fruits, and vegetables, specifically, leafy greens. The greater the variety of vegetables, fruits, nuts, and beans you consume, the healthier your overall diet. The greater the variety of whole foods you consume, the more essential vitamins and minerals your body will take in. Also, eating vitamins and minerals in their natural form, from healthy foods, rather than taking supplements, allows the digestive system to utilize them more efficiently. Such eating also reduces the risk of artificially ingesting an excess of any particular vitamin or mineral, which could lead to other problems, such as blood poisoning or kidney stones. Also, the National Cancer Institute supports five servings of vegetables and fruit daily for the reduction of several types of cancers. Marion Nestle, the chair of the Department of Nutrition, Food Studies, and Public Health at New York University, in her book *Food Politics,* said this regarding whole foods:

> As an academic nutritionist, I grapple on a daily basis with what I see as a central contradiction between nutrition theory and practice. On the one hand, our advice about the health benefits of diets based largely on food

plants—fruits, vegetables, and grains—has not changed in more than fifty years and is consistently supported by ongoing research. On the other hand, people seem increasingly confused about what they are supposed to eat to stay healthy. As a population, Americans are eating more animal-based foods—and more food in general—to the point where half of us are overweight, even our children are obese, and diseases related to diet are leading causes of death and disability.[19]

Consider the story of Daniel in the Old Testament. When Daniel was appointed by the king of Babylon to his royal service, he was given the same diet of all the people of the palace. His rations were to be that of the wealthy, royal rations of food and wine. As with all prosperous kings' tables at the time, royal rations meant nothing but the finest fatted calves and pork and much of it. Daniel suggested to the palace master to let him have only vegetables and water to eat while the rest of the royal servants ate the heavy animal-based foods from the royal table. The palace master, who feared the king, was afraid of the effects that only vegetables and water would have on Daniel. But Daniel talked him into a contest of ten days allowing him to eat only vegetables and water, while everyone else ate the rich foods and drank fine wine (probably the first documented weight-loss challenge). After ten days, Daniel was remarkably healthier than those who ate the fatty foods. So much so that the palace master ordered the vegetable diet for all the servants of the royal palace.

There is a phenomenon that is noted in research regarding affluence and nutrition. Marion Nestle calls this the "nutrition transition." As emerging nations become more and more prosperous, they tend to leave the dominant plant-based diets for more animal-based diets, complete with heavy processing, refined sugars and flours, and lots of animal fat. This, of course, starts the cycle of rapid weight gain and chronic disease. The irony is that, if the individuals were to continue with the plant-based rations, they would be much better off physically in spite of being a "prosperous" nation.

The American diet contains huge quantities of refined sugars, processed flours, and heavy animal fats. It is obvious that such a diet was never intended for human consumption on a regular basis.

> A self-indulgent man lives to eat; a self-restrained man eats to live.[20]
> —Mahatma Gandhi

Nutritional and caloric needs vary with each individual. An individual's muscle mass (size) and activity level will affect needs. The current RDA of 2,000 calories might seem a bit high to start with, but men who are heavily-muscled and active could have a caloric intake need of much more than that amount, while inactive small-framed women might require fewer calories in a day.

The individual must find his or her own caloric need. Understanding the difference between want and true need is critical. Feeling hunger pangs may not be a sign of needing immediate calories. Pangs, sluggishness, fatigue, and dizziness might be signs of the need for more calories, but it could also be symptoms of dehydration or blood-sugar variations. By listening closely to your body you can become more in tune with needs and avoid feeding wants. Rather than struggling to count calories, be real about what you consume in a day. You will see in time that being tuned into need instead of want is much more beneficial than straight calorie counting. As we will discuss, you will be surprised on how filling a diet rich in vegetables, fruit, and whole grains can be. You may also be shocked at the enormous volume of food you actually need to eat with a primarily plant-based diet as opposed to a highly processed, animal-based diet.

An interesting study by Elizabeth Bell, Ph.D., and researchers at Pennsylvania State University recently used as the base research for the book, *Volumetrics: Weight-Control Plan*,[21] found that healthy women instinctively ate around the same volume or amount of food a day and it didn't matter whether it was high or low in calories. The weight of the food in a day remained the constant; the quantity of food, and not the calories, satisfies one's desire to eat. In other words, if we ate equal amounts of healthy whole foods of lower calories in a day, we would more likely satisfy our desire long-term than if we were to eat less volume of unhealthy, processed, higher calorie foods. Fruits and vegetables, like us humans, are made up of primarily water, which adds tremendous volume with no extra calories. We will discuss this in detail in the next chapter. Food volume might also be some insight as to why diets usually end up broken after a period of time. The desire for a certain amount of food instinctively overrides the desire to lose weight. To learn to eat and be filled with larger amounts of whole foods might make certain a lifetime of proper nutrition and will naturally battle obesity in the long run.

Studies in the American Journal of Clinical Nutrition between 1990 and 2002 reveal that drinking sugar-rich drinks, such as regular soda, did not curb the appetite of a person throughout the day. Those drinking non-caloric drinks and those drinking sugar-rich drinks ate the same volume of food. It is clear that drinking sugar-rich drinks will add to obesity by adding extra calories, but doing nothing to the overall desire for the volume of food in a day.

The conclusion is to not waste your calories in a day on things like sugar-rich drinks, or processed or low-nutrition foods. Save calories and volume of food for healthy, low-calorie, fiber-rich, whole food that will satisfy cravings by eating all you want. This will satisfy overall hunger and nutritional needs.

Dr. Fuhrman, M.D., author of *Eat to Live,* coined a wonderful formula. It determines the Nutrient Density of food choices.[22] The formula says that health is equal to the nutrients you eat divided by the calories:

Health = Nutrients/Calories

Simply put, the more nutrient-rich foods we eat that are low in calories, the better our health. Vegetables, which have extremely high nutrients for low calories, fit Dr. Fuhrman's formula very well. Fruit also has very high nutrients and fiber with enormous water content. Whole grains and beans are high in nutrients and fiber. Meats, refined sugars, and flours have lower overall nutrients and more calories. We can see that a diet rich in plant-based foods has greater nutrients and fewer calories than the animal-based and processed-food diets that are popular in America today.

We are overly trained about food do's and don'ts. But focusing on food still keeps our attention on food. Striving for a balanced diet, Americans consume large amounts of vitamin supplements, prepackaged food bars, and nutritional shakes. Here, too, we have created so many things artificially to mimic what has been given to us naturally. A nutrition bar that has 320 calories could have a well-balanced set of nutrients and fiber. Ironically, you can eat about 110 asparagus spears to equal the same calories but with more protein, dietary fiber, vitamins A and C, calcium, iron, potassium, and with less fat and sodium. Eating 110 asparagus spears will certainly be more filling than a nutrition bar, just not quite as tasty. The same is true for green beans. Calories in one bar equal about ten cups of green beans; or with tomatoes, one bar equals about nine tomatoes. The calories from one bar equals four apples, three bananas, three pears, or eight cups of watermelon. All the mentioned fruits and vegetables have more fiber and less sodium and fat than that nutrition bar. Of course, this is a nutrition bar comparison to natural foods. Let's compare fast food with natural foods.

A Big Mac™, with 590 calories, is equal to about 190 asparagus spears. The burger has 34 grams of fat, while asparagus has zero. As you can see, it isn't that we do not have healthier choices; it is the choices we make.

Rather than eating three large meals throughout the day, eat three smaller meals and a few healthy snacks.

That change will improve digestion, regulate metabolism, prevent sluggishness, and stabilize the release of insulin. With lower insulin in the blood, you run a lesser risk of developing insulin resistance, Type II diabetes, and other health problems. Since insulin is the body's fat storage hormone, less insulin means less stored fat. With less insulin, more body fat can be metabolized for energy.

Healthy choices of high-nutrient, low-calorie foods have been with us always. Giving thanks for food we are about to partake in can motivate us to be gracious and conservative in our eating.

Questions to Ponder

In what sense are natural foods created for us by design? How does that understanding Creator and creation change your perspective on the food choices you make?

Living Water

> For in the one Spirit we were all baptized into one body—Jews or Greeks, slaves or free—and we were all made to drink of one Spirit.
> —1 Corinthians 12:13

Christ often uses the image of water in his message of salvation. In John 4, he describes himself as living water, "Those who drink of the water I will give him will never be thirsty" (John 4:14). The Samaritan woman to whom he speaks wished to know more about this water.

Shunned by the Jewish community as a Samaritan, she is a sinful outsider with unacceptable religious beliefs, and also, she has had many husbands. It is not surprising that this hopeless sinner accepts Jesus' gift of living water, and begins to tell others about this life-changing water.

Baptism into new life is with water. Rain is celebrated as life-giving. Throughout history, farmers have prayed for the one variable that can determine the difference between feast and famine—rain. Water is what sustains us and brings us life.

The human body is about 75 percent water. Blood is about 94 percent water. Water is, without a doubt, an appropriate metaphor for life. Some researchers estimate that the changes in our diets from real fruits and vegetables to processed foods, and our higher consumption of drinks like soda, coffee, and alcohol have a clear effect on our bodies. Real fruits and vegetables contain mostly water, like us humans. Alcohol and caffeine found in coffee and soda are diuretics that stimulate an increase in urine output. Processed foods are primarily dehydrated for better shipping and storage. Our nation's current diet encourages little water intake. We are a nation that is suffering from chronic dehydration. We lack living water.

Water is not only important to every aspect of life, but it also aids digestion and adds bulk to food. Living things, like fruits and vegetables, all are sustained by and contain large quantities of water. The closer to the original version of the whole food, the more water it contains. Even though a raisin and a grape have equal calories, the water content makes the difference. The original form of the grape has much greater volume causing a feeling of satisfaction after eating the same amount of calories as the raisin. The grape has nearly eight times the volume or bulk than the raisin and with equal nutrients, plus grapes have a significantly lower Glycemic Index number than raisins.

When fresh whole fruits and vegetables come off the vine or tree and are eaten before any processing, they cause a more full feeling with equal calories than versions of the same fruit or vegetable that have either been dehydrated or stripped of their fiber. The contrast is even more dramatic when comparing fresh whole fruits and vegetables to manufactured, processed foods. Real whole, fresh fruits and vegetables contain a large percentage of water—healthy and filling water that aids digestion, adds bulk, curbs the appetite, and gives life.

In his book, *Water for Health, for Healing, for Life,* Dr. F. Batmanghelidj identifies forty-six reasons why the body needs ample water every day. The list includes water being the medium that transports all substances inside the body, its contribution to the prevention of obesity, and its role in decreasing joint and lower back pain.[23]

Water is the source for all life. It is God's gift. Lack of clean water is, and will continue to be, the most immediate threat to the lives of the very poor. By limiting the water we use for tasks that do not directly involve drinking or growing food (such as overwatering lawns and washing cars), we not only save our own money, but we show compassion to our neighbors by better using our resources.

Giving thanks for clean water is a wonderful practice. It reminds us to conserve and strive to make sure everyone has it. Such a life-giving gift must be shared. One of the most powerful and important mission projects is the building of a village well that can bring water for drinking and for crops. A well can restore life.

When Henry David Thoreau speaks of diet, he mentions that he eats only the simplest foods and refuses all alcoholic drinks because they might ruin his taste for water.[24] Like the Samaritan woman at the well, let us all eagerly receive the living water so we will not thirst again.

Questions to Ponder
What dramatic experiences have you had
with water—or a lack of it? How can you and your
community conserve water in very practical ways?

Price of Affluence

And he, who supplies seed to the sower and bread for
food, will supply and multiply your seed for sowing
and increase the harvest of your righteousness.
   —2 Corinthians 9:10

Are you ready to buy into the monumental shift from the need-to-lose-weight paradigm to the need-to-feed-others paradigm? We have already explored the fact that we are spending billions to help us curb our appetites while our neighbors have nothing. We realize the injustice of this, but what can we do about it? Looking a little deeper at this problem might help us move to action.

Do not underestimate your ability to make changes that make a difference. Compassionate awareness has brought about world changes of great magnitude. The U. S. economy is the largest in the world. As global consumers, we carry a power that can facilitate change. By our collective efforts we can influence each other, businesses, and governments. Our efforts do not have to be so extreme. Supplying goods at the lowest cost possible to beat the competitor's prices for the consumer is what business in a free market does. This is how a free market works. When we, as consumers, do not ask questions, or we make purchases based strictly on the cost or desire, we may be inviting the evils of labor exploitation, deforestation, or unfair treatment of resources in order to get the lowest cost of a product. As consumers, we have to become responsible for the purchases we make. Business, by design, will rise to meet the demands of the consumer. It is up to us, individually and collectively, to demand goods that are offered with a social, environmental, and health consciousness. It is in our best interest and the best interest of our neighbors that we start to look past the attractive advertisements and look more deeply into the truth of our own food consumption.

The United States Department of Agriculture (USDA) economists estimate that eating more fruit and vegetables and fewer foods of animal origin would upset the existing "volume, mix, production, and marketing of agricultural commodities" and would require large "adjustments" in international food trade, nonfood uses of basic commodities, and food prices.[25] Can America afford to switch its diet away from heavily processed, sugared, and animal-based diets to a more whole, natural, plant-based diet? The question posed in this chapter is, "Can America afford not to?"

The average American child sees 10,000 food ads a year on television, and 95 percent of them are for sugared cereals, fast food, soft drinks, and candy.[26] My kids and I watch cartoons occasionally. The other day, during a half hour segment we counted sixteen commercials, eight of them for junk food or restaurants that served junk food. Although I have a fairly strong defense against such temptations, I found myself hungry for those high-fat, high-calorie, salty snacks. I can only imagine how most eight-year-olds feel after a couple hours of that temptation.

At least 64 percent of Americans are either overweight or obese, with the number growing. The increase in overweight children is twice that seen in adults.[27] In the last three decades, childhood obesity has increased two- to three-fold.[28]

An interesting study of Canadian Mennonite children might provide a little insight into the development of the recent epidemic of our overweight children. The study shows that a traditional way of life—that is, physical labor and physical play—may reduce chronic disease. The results of the study suggest that children who live a lifestyle somewhat representative of previous generations (Mennonite lifestyle: no television, video games, or processed foods) are leaner and stronger than children living a contemporary Canadian lifestyle.[29] In other words, the sedentary behaviors adopted by our current lifestyles have mostly contributed to the obesity epidemic in our children. During the agricultural age, labor was physical and play was outdoors. Yesterday's rope swing and physical games have been replaced, for the majority of adolescents, by the video game and television. The fruits and vegetables from the fields of a hundred years ago are replaced with today's processed combo meals.

Richard Louv, author of *Last Child in the Woods,* came to disturbing conclusions in his work with adolescents. He discovered that the recent switch from outdoor (natural) play to indoor television and video games are linked directly to the trends of childhood obesity, Attention Deficit Disorder (ADD), and depression.[30]

Most experts agree that it is the sedentary lifestyle of passive television, computers, video games, and processed foods that are to blame for the increase in obese children. Of all the reasons listed why youth are becoming obese at this epidemic proportion, television is the catalyst that receives the greatest blame. Let's take a closer look at why television might be in line for the number-one cause of childhood obesity.

First, television requires no activity. In fact, it is arguable that REM (Rapid Eye Movement) sleep for a child can burn more calories and invokes more activity than watching television. Second, during television programs, especially during the shows designed for children, the majority of the commercials are designed to young people for sugared cereals, fast foods, snack foods, soft drinks, and candy. Third, boredom provokes snacking. Television is the least active event in a youth's day, even less active than sleeping and dreaming. Snacking is most often a result of boredom and not hunger. The sedentary lifestyle directly increases snacking of unhealthy foods that are being marketed during the hours of boredom watching television. It is a vicious cycle for our young people—a cycle that is costing them their health.

In addition to affecting our health, processed foods greatly affect our environment. In his movie *SuperSize Me,* Morgan Spurlock said:

> McDonald's feeds forty-six million people a day, and the garbage from one day at McDonald's is enough to fill the Empire State Building; and that's just one fast food chain.[31]

It is not just the garbage we toss in our trash cans, but also the hidden garbage. For every ton of trash we throw away, there was considerably more "manufacturing and industrial" waste produced to make that product.

Elizabeth Royte, the author of *Garbage Land*, adds, "if we don't wake up and make the connection between our economy and the environment (which provides the resources to make all our stuff), the planet will eventually do it for us. And it won't be pretty."[32]

Additional paper, plastic, tin, aluminum, and glass products are used directly through food processing and packaging. Much can be done about the waste we produce with the foods we choose. A bag of fresh local fruit, vegetables, or beans could produce one recyclable plastic bag. The whole food goes from the harvest to the local consumer for sale. Processed foods run through a chain of conversions, travel, and middlemen until they eventually emerge as the product. As cheap meats, refined sugars, and flours are demanded from the consumer (as in fast food burgers), the topsoil, water, fossil fuels, and rainforests have all been affected by the current American diet.

Rich, healthy soil is disappearing. I didn't fully understand this until I visited the experimental farm at The

Rodale Institute in Kutztown, Pennsylvania. The Rodale Institute is a non-profit side of Rodale, Inc., which publishes popular wellness magazines like *Prevention, Runner's World,* and *Men's Health.* The Rodale Institute's ongoing soil, farming, and produce research is showing how we are all affected by the farming industrial methods. The founder, J. I. Rodale, who originally coined the term *organic farming,* was dedicated to the natural relationship we have to the soil. The Rodale Institute's motto is simple: Healthy soil = Healthy food = Healthy people.

Since 1981, Rodale has been comparing organic and conventional grain-based farming systems. Through the use of heavy, conventional, manufactured fertilizers, herbicides, insecticides, and fungicides, our food, soil, and ecosystem have changed since the birth of the modern farming techniques after World War II.

The research, which is now in its third decade, reveals that by restoring nutrients to the soil naturally through organic methods of composting, crop rotations, cover crops, and more natural biodiversity, the farming environment is more apt to conserve soil, water, energy, and biological resources,[33] while adding nutrients to the crops.

Composting adds a richer organic soil matter (carbon and nitrogen) which helps conserve water resources, and soil becomes more drought resistant. Employing natural biodiversity eliminates the need to use manufactured nitrogen fertilizers, herbicides, insecticides, and fungicides.

In essence, using farming techniques that have been around for six thousand years helps to restore the nutrients in the produce and in the environment. In a sense, it also provides stability for a farming future without manufactured fertilizers, herbicides, insecticides, and fungicides.

Visiting the Rodale farm is a powerful experience that cannot be communicated on paper. The farm concentrates on the soil as it was intended to be. When we take care of the soil, it will take care of us. The ongoing studies reveal something that we already know through faith: God provides naturally. We are called to be good stewards of the soil that we have been given.

> In an era of fast food, it is extremely important that we take time to rediscover the spiritual value of food. Cultivate eating as an opportunity to express humble gratitude for the abundance we experience in our lives. In addition, when we eat with those we are close to, eating has even special meaning far beyond calories and nutrients . . . savor that moment. "Dear Lord, thank you for this daily bread and all the efforts of those who have brought it to this table. Let me and mine be of Thy service. Amen."
> —Paul Reed Hepperly, Ph.D., Research Manager, The Rodale Institute[34]

When you walk around the 333-acre Rodale Institute farmland, you get a feeling of optimism. It is a realization that if people were given a chance, we would collectively right the wrongs of the way we treat our land because of our current appetites. This feeling is also present for similar reasons when you visit the ECHO demonstration farm in North Fort Myers, Florida.

ECHO (Educational Concerns for Hunger Organization), is a fifty-five-acre laboratory that has a plethora of displays demonstrating living situations in the tropical Third World. ECHO's objective is to help those working internationally with the poor to be more effective, especially in the area of agriculture.[35]

Some of the solutions to the problems that Third World countries face that are addressed at ECHO are: rooftop farming in heavily populated urban areas where ground is scarce; terracing, where the natural terrain is not farmable; farming in rainforests, in monsoon regions, and arid regions; and solutions to bad soil using natural resources. The mission of ECHO is solving problems. They offer possibilities that seem impossible, such as ways of trapping rainwater and planting using abandoned garbage. They educate missionaries to the 180 countries that are in desperate need of stable agriculture.

When I visit ECHO, I get that same feeling of hope that I get at the Rodale Institute. There is something so pure and spiritual about caring for the soil—that feeling of graciousness, knowing that we all live because of our nurturing relationship with the earth. When we do not experience this relationship, we run the risk of treating the earth like we are its masters. We take and take and eventually run it out of business.

> God said, "See, I have given you every plant yielding seed that is upon the face of all the earth, and every tree with seed in its fruit; you shall have them for food."
> —Genesis 1:29

Since the great majority of the corn and grain that is farmed in the United States goes to feed livestock (approximately 70 percent of grain[36] and 80 percent of corn[37]), it would make sense that livestock is responsible for the majority of the water that is used directly on the crops for growing. In fact, the majority of the water used from wells and aquifers in America does go to crops for feed. If the same crops (or other types of vegetables) were given directly to humans for consumption instead of given to livestock, the efficiency of food volume would be greatly increased. Vegetables, fruits, legumes, and whole grains eaten directly by humans create a great deal more volume of food compared to feeding it to cattle and then eating the meat. Likewise, the ratio of water use per volume of healthier food would go down significantly. From one acre of land, 250 pounds of beef can be produced. From one acre, 40,000 pounds of potatoes or onions can be harvested. In one acre 30,000 pounds of carrots, 50,000 pounds of tomatoes, or 60,000 pounds of celery can be produced.[38] Vegetables and grain can be grown in a fraction of the space needed for beef. It is estimated that the livestock in the United States eat enough grain and soybeans to feed the entire population of the country five times over.[39] Clearly, the food selections we make determine, in part, our battle with obesity while also not utilizing our resources to their full capacity.

Higher density feedlots create more meat in less space. But, the high volume of manure in a concentrated area causes both a soil imbalance and an increased need for antibiotics for the animals. Currently, we ingest more traces of animal antibiotics, pesticides, and fertilizers than fifty years ago. The demand has risen consistently for inexpensive meats over the past half century. It is the demand for unhealthy, cheap meats that has pushed commercial farmers to supply the current demand while staying at competitive prices.

In addition to degrading our soil, current farming techniques have also consumed our fossil fuels at a higher rate than fifty years ago. With mass commercial farming and the large consumption of prepackaged processed foods, food products are grown miles from where they are sold. The journey begins in the fields, and then to the processing plants, to packaging, and then to the stores or fast food restaurants for the consumer. Fossil fuels are used at an enormous rate for the shipping of food and food products to different destinations. Consumers, especially those living in cities, have very little knowledge of local growers or the growing seasons of local foods. Farmer's markets, roadside stands, and local farming cooperatives could allow the consumer fresher, less expensive, and healthier whole foods at peak seasons. This reduces the cost of shipping, packaging, and processing, in addition to all the health advantages to whole foods while supporting local farmers in the process. Often the local farmer is the one reimbursed the least for his or her efforts.

Fossil fuels are also used in greater concentrations to produce the conventional farming fertilizers, insecticides, and weed killers that organic farming does not. Fossil fuels are not unlimited resources, yet over the last fifty years, our use and dependency of these fuels had exponentially increased.

We have looked at how the current food market affects our country's natural resources. Now let's take a step back and look at a more global picture. An area of recent focus has been the rainforests.

The rainforests provide natural habitats to thousands of plant and animal species, as well as help toward stablizing global climate. But our world's rainforests are being destroyed at an astounding rate. Beyond all of the natural resources we do lose as the rainforests shrink, that loss is also affecting the global climate.

First, it seems that global warming is caused by an accumulation of heat-trapping gases (such as carbon dioxide and carbon monoxide) that are emitted from the burning of fossil fuels such as coal, oil, and gasoline. Second, it is enhanced by a reduction of overall trees and plant life in the world. Carbon dioxide becomes more prevalent the more fossil fuels are burned, the more artificial fertilizers are used on crops and the fewer trees there are. To simplify, humans breathe in air to utilize the oxygen, then exhale carbon dioxide. Trees and plants, for the most part, do the opposite. Trees utilize heat-trapping carbon dioxide and emit oxygen. We were created to live in harmony with trees and plants, but the evidence suggests that the increased burning of fossil fuels and the destruction of the world's rainforests throws off the symbiosis of our ecosystem, and the result is a slightly higher carbon-gas-rich atmosphere that traps heat and causes the weather to warm-up globally. So between having fewer trees, more burned fossil fuels, and heavy use of manufactured fertilizers, the natural state of the atmosphere is affected.

What happens to the land after the vegetation is removed rarely involves a large replanting effort. The lumber from the rainforest is sold and the majority of the stripped land is used in other ways. Most of the land is used to grow corn and grain for livestock. As the demand for beef increases, so does the need for rich inexpensive land for raising livestock. The native people live off the resources of the rainforest. Without the rainforests, people (and native animals) lose their food resources. In addition to reducing the effects of global warming, the rainforests need to be protected for the natural resources they provide the indigenous people who rely on their vegetation and canopy.

If we were to make a healthy shift toward resources which harvest directly from what already exists in the rainforests (medicinal plants, natural fruit, nuts, rubber products, coffee, and cocoa beans), we could maintain the ecosystem of our neighbors' lands while providing a fair, ongoing income for those poorer countries based on the natural resources they have.

Some companies, like Ben & Jerry's Homemade, Inc., have raised public awareness of the shrinking rainforests and have become proactive in the battle to save them by using the natural resources that the rainforests provide (vanilla extract, cashews, and Brazilian nuts).[40] In addition, many faith-based agencies and businesses have become aware of the value of maintaining nature and selling the goods without interrupting the ecosystem. Coffee, tea, cocoa, and chocolate are traded through the Equal Exchange food co-op. This organization and others like it supply farmers with a fair market, consistent price for their products, while maintaining the natural resources and leaving ecosystems intact by supporting the growth of "shaded" organic coffee. This shaded coffee grows in its natural environment without the use of pesticides. The International Fair Trade Association is a good resource that networks socially, environmentally, and medically sound organizations together with consumers who don't base their purchases on cost alone, but on value and compassion as well.

Questions to Ponder
How do you make food choices? How does
your current diet affect your global neighbors?

Feed My Sheep

> And the king will answer them, 'Truly I tell you, just
> as you did it to one of the least of these who are mem-
> bers of my family, you did it to me."
> —Matthew 25:40

In 1963, President John F. Kennedy stated to congress,
"We have the ability, we have the means, and we have
the capacity to eliminate hunger from the face of the
earth in our lifetime. We need only the will."[41]

More recently in 2006, Jeffrey D. Sachs the author
of *The End of Poverty,* made clear that extreme poverty
could be eliminated forever with the involvement of the
global community.

Think about it. What if the shift from the current
need-to-lose-weight paradigm to the need-to-feed-others
paradigm really were to happen? This nation would lose
weight more easily. More importantly, we would feed the
poor.

What if our consumption patterns were to change
from buying food based only on lowest cost or preferred
tastes to a focus on the companies that are socially, environmentally, and health conscious? We could end world
hunger, restore healthy soil, decrease use of excessive
pesticides and artificial fertilizers, reduce burning of
fossil fuels, stop deforestation, supply stable income to

impoverished farmers and reverse the obesity epidemic in wealthy nations. It is estimated that reducing Americans' meat consumption by only 10 percent, could feed sixty million people with the grains saved.[42] This is "loving our neighbor" while helping ourselves live healthier lives. Such statistics may seem extreme, but just remember, you can feed many times more people with the vegetables, beans, whole grains, and fruit grown on a piece of land than you can one meat-eater.

God made it simple; humans make it complicated. Eat a moderate amount of fruit, vegetables, whole grains, nuts, lean proteins and/or beans, and discover how fulfilling that can be. The nutritional value of these things that are given to us naturally has no comparison to processed food. One meal of hamburger, fries, and soda could be equal in calories to twenty-five apples, or thirty oranges, or a bucket of carrots, peppers, cauliflower, lettuce, asparagus, green beans, and broccoli. Although it is humanly impossible to eat a bucket of vegetables in one sitting, the calorie content would be similar to that fast food mentioned, but it would contain less fat, more nutrients and much, much greater volume.

The extra dietary fiber and water content from whole foods creates the bulk that satiates the appetite and regulates the gastrointestinal system—with reduced risk of cancers and related intestinal problems. The other nutritional virtues of whole foods are too numerous to mention here. Just keep in mind that,

> Food is best off the vine, from the land and out
>   of the sea;
> As whole and natural as it was intended to be.

There is some good news. Our nation shows strong trends toward recycling and even composting, and is developing an acute awareness of food facts. There is also an increase in numbers of organic farms around the country.

This might be a good place to mention a commonly held misconception related to global poverty. Too many people ask, "Doesn't starvation keep the populations down in those countries that are overpopulated anyway? If we feed everyone, won't the population just grow to an unmanageable number?" Absolutely not! Poverty actually contributes to population explosions in the Third World. Let's put this myth that "poverty is necessary for population control" to bed once and for all.

The populations of thriving, developed countries typically have a steady number of births and deaths. In recent years, populations have actually shown a decline in the wealthy nations. Underdeveloped countries—countries with limited government infrastructures—like schools, electricity, maintained roads, and healthcare—have more children born per mother. We can trace these trends in birth rate directly to several factors, and all of them have to do with poverty.

First of all, impoverished children die in large numbers.[43] Women give birth to more children to compensate for the increased infant mortality. Secondly, as a society moves from an agricultural base to urban settings, the need for many children diminishes. Upgraded farming equipment and stable working conditions mean families need the labor of fewer children.[44] Third, improved healthcare leads to more surviving infants, greatly reducing the need for pregnancies. Healthcare also introduces birth control methods and, finally, education! The more access women have to education—learning about trades, reproductive choices, and good health—the fewer children are born. Parents who can choose the size of their families will have the time and energy to invest in their children—along with a commitment to their education. Jeffrey Sachs, in *The End of Poverty,* adds,

> All of these factors explain why most of the world has achieved a marked reduction of total fertility rates and a sharp slowdown in population growth.[45]

With a disciplined consciousness about our eating and with a compassion for our hungry neighbors, we will solve the epidemic of obesity and the shameful imbalance of world hunger, control the population explosions of the Third World, and move away from further destruction of our environment.

This sounds ambitious—and it is. But the choices we privileged consumers make have awesome consequences. This is truly "food for thought."

Questions to Ponder
Who are the sheep Jesus commands us to feed?
Because Jesus identifies himself as "the least
of these," where do I see the face of Jesus today?

Food

Ninety percent produce: Compared to a current heavy animal-based processed diet, a majority plant-based diet (90 percent of the overall calories in a day being non-animal calories), consisting of a variety of vegetables, fruits, whole grains, beans, nuts, and seeds would reduce heart disease, hypertension, risk of stroke, diabetes, obesity, cancer, and other such health problems directly linked to excessive fats, refined sugars, and processed flours. Healthcare cost would flatten, saving Medicare and extending a healthier life for the individual.

Seasonal produce, local growers: Food that currently travels an average of thirteen hundred miles from the farm, through the processing factories, to the consumer would be reduced indefinitely. The dependence on fossil fuels would be dramatically reduced nationwide. Pollution and global warming would decline. Local growers, small farms, would be supported.

Waste: Garbage produced (4.5 pounds per human each day[46] from food and drink processing and packaging would be reduced by more than 50 percent. The organic skins, peels, and shells from the produce eaten can be directly returned to enrich the soil through composting in a personal, church, or community garden. The majority of the overall drinkable water used today goes directly to the fields to grow feed for livestock. Changing the nation to a predominately plant-based diet from an animal-based diet would be one of the single most effective ways to conserve drinkable water, our most precious and disappearing resource.

High-density feedlots would decline. Also, rainforest destruction would diminish due to less demand for cattle grazing and an increase demand for the natural resources the forest provides.

The current American diet, with over half of the daily calories coming from animal products (beef, poultry, cheese, eggs, and dairy) could be improved considerably with personal health, weight loss, and environmental benefit by replacing the animal-based foods with plant-based, whole, non-processed, locally grown foods such as leafy green vegetables, fruits, nuts, seeds, beans, and whole grains.

Chapter 3: Exercise

We have found the fountain of youth: it's exercise. Think about how you will be living the last twenty years of your life. Exercise today will have a tremendous effect on those years. The magic of the fountain of youth is that it keeps you younger even as you get older.[1]

—Covert Bailey, *The New Fit or Fat*

Exercise for Life

You are unique. You never were before. You never will be again. You are wonderfully created with certain quirks, habits, interests, hobbies, and most importantly, gifts to offer the world—truly unique gifts that only you can give.

The reality of our uniqueness had initially come clear to me in the fall of 1987. I was in human anatomy class in which I had the opportunity to perform my first cadaver dissection. It was the miracle of the body that convinced me there is great value in taking care of ourselves. I have had the privilege and honor of performing nearly twenty dissections since 1987. Each time I enter that rarely-seen world of the human body, I stand and marvel.

Of this I'm sure: we cannot fully grasp the miracle that we are at first glance. The language we use to describe the body speaks of systems and cells, but we are limited in our full understanding. We speak of diseases in old age, but we miss the wonder of many years of good health. We are carefully planned, thought through in every loving detail. The human body is wonderfully made; it is God's greatest creation. In our search for miracles, one needs only look under one's own skin to see the greatest miracle. Life cannot be explained without a creator, both loving and with a purpose. We are not the result of chance. In the search for meaning, I think Edward Abbey said it best: "Only petty minds and trivial souls yearn for supernatural events, incapable of perceiving that everything—everything!—within and around them is pure miracle."[2]

It would become my deepest passion to convince others to care for the marvelous creation they have been given—the human body. We are no genetic mistake. We are made for significance, carefully created and intricately detailed. We have the capacity to imagine, reason, and create. The simple movement of a muscle requires an absolute orchestra of chemicals and electrical charges, carefully timed and choreographed. Simultaneous inhibition of the opposing muscles needs to be timed appropriately, unless of course, the brain decides to contract the muscle at a rapid rate by releasing more chemicals than the opposing muscles need to contract while lengthening only at a perfect rate so the muscle will not tear. And this, of course, is only the abridged version of the muscular system functioning during a single muscle contraction. And while this goes on, every other system in the body cooperates to make it happen. It is easy to overlook a miracle when it is you.

Now it is time for a third and final paradigm shift or change in belief. To review, in the first chapter, we discussed a change in belief that was taught to us by contented senior adults. This change in belief is to simplify our lives and allow love (not money or anything else) to be the primary motivator for our actions. In the end, contented elderly agree that love is what makes a life that was worth living. The second paradigm shift was to change from the current need-to-lose-weight model toward a need-to-feed-others model. With this thinking, this nation would lose weight more easily. More importantly, we would feed the poor. The third and final shift is to care for yourself to better care for others, through the discipline of exercise. Ultimately, all three shifts in our thinking involve a monumental step; allowing love and compassion to be the catalyst for our motivation to serve the global community through diet and exercise.

I can do all things through him who strengthens me.
    —Philippians 4:13

It is 10 A.M. at the Sports Medicine and Wellness Center in Cape Coral, Florida. Rudy prepares to complete his second of three sets on the leg press. Rudy has just turned ninety-eight years old. He has deliberately exercised every day that he can remember. Eighty years ago, he was in military school. It was between the World Wars. He always said "I was too young for World War I, but too old for World War II."

He remembers leading his men in hikes. He remembers lifting weights (back then it was medicine balls) eighty years ago, and the habit never stopped. He ran the 100-yard dash in the 1924 Olympics in Paris in 10.75 seconds. Rudy had observed the birth of the automobile, airplane, and the X ray. He was an adult when the first television was invented. At eighty years old, he had to quit running because it started to be hard on his arthritic right knee. Eighteen years later, he continues to do strength training and walking. Rudy feels that you need to work out with consistency or else you can't move at all. He would say "You get rusty if you don't exercise every day." Rudy always ate healthy from the farm. He never picked up unhealthy habits like excessive drinking or smoking.

This is the missing link. Our fitness and diet industry has pursued physical appearance, youth, or aesthetics as the primary motivation for exercise and healthy eating. Although a strong motivator in the earlier years of life, physical appearance alone cannot and will not motivate an individual into a lifestyle of exercise, health-conscious eating, and non-destructive habits for an entire lifetime. Life is so much more than appearance. Jesus said, "Is not life more than food, and the body more than clothing?" (Matthew 6:25).

Finishing his third set on the leg press, Rudy takes a deserved break. With direct eye contact and a hand on my shoulder he says, "Thank you." You see, Rudy affirms others. He commits himself fully to his relationships. He is a Christian disciple who understands his calling. He is thankful for every day. Rarely does he speak of his own struggles or his own pain even though they exist. Being contented is a conscious choice. It is refusing to be self-absorbed in one's own limitations or self-pity. It is making the decision to "aspire to love."

Rudy understands this motivation. His disciplined life of exercise and healthy habits is a direct connection to his spiritual health.

"We have found the fountain of youth: it's exercise." The body is a miracle; it can heal and strengthen with a disciplined exercise program that addresses aging problems and fitness. Adhering closely to exercise and proper nutrition will increase the chances for an individual to remain disability-free until the end of life.

The majority of the body's decline is due not to the passing of years, but to the combined efforts of inactivity, poor nutrition, and illness, much of which can be controlled. Regardless of age or present physical condition, the aging process can be slowed and—often times—even reversed.

Consider the following as you look at how the body works. Rigorous exercises and physical work do not break down muscle, bone, heart, and lungs, but actually build them up. They improve the body's efficiency. Do you feel that God created us to be active? In fact, did God intend for us to be very active? Remember, hunting, gathering, and primitive farming were all part of our original occupations of extremely heavy labor. It has only been the last century when our jobs became sedentary.

In the book, *Successful Aging,* a ten-year study uncovered a solid truth of aging: declining physical function is preventable and reversible.[3] Regular exercise slows the natural aging process by the following: bones strengthen (reversing osteoporosis), muscle atrophy diminishes (reversing sarcopenia), arthritis formation slows, body fat reduces (reversing obesity), posture improves, the immune system strengthens, short-term memory in elderly improves, cardiovascular output increases, the risk of many cancers and diabetes diminishes, sleep patterns regulate, relaxation improves, muscle balance and coordination in the elderly improves, hypertension decreases, depression and anxiety reduce, and self image improves. Exercise is also linked to protecting against Alzheimer's disease.

Questions to Ponder

In what sense is life defined as movement? What can I improve in my daily life with regular exercise?

Exercise as Medicine

Our current American health care costs us about 15.5 percent of our total spending (Gross National Product).[4] Of this, about $200 billion is spent on prescription drugs.[5] These numbers have risen astronomically in the last twenty years. Also, in 1993 the average number of prescriptions written per person in a year was seven. In 2004, it was twelve.[6] Most of those drugs are taken by senior citizens, and of those drugs, the majority are taken for chronic conditions, like arthritic pain, osteoporosis, heart disease, hypertension, depression, and diabetes. As the baby-boomers age, this expense is expected to become dramatically higher.

As we learned in the food chapter, we are spending roughly 13 percent of all our GNP in America on food and the food industry, or about one trillion dollars.

The estimate is that about 3,800 calories are produced daily per person in America with this expense. This is almost twice the number of calories we need! If we add our healthcare costs and our food costs together (15.5 percent and 13 percent respectively), we can see that for every dollar spent in America, more than a quarter goes to food and health care. Knowing what we know regarding the chronic conditions mentioned above (arthritis, osteoporosis, heart disease, hypertension, depression, and diabetes), what role might exercise play in reducing the need for prescription medications? Can exercise prevent premature disability or a shortened life as a result of these ailments that tend to plague senior citizens?

Without question, exercise has a role in slowing the development of almost all early disability or life-threatening ailments. And the single most important step we can take as a nation to secure our healthcare system is to start eating healthier and exercising faithfully today.

Exercise and arthritis: Osteoarthritis (generally called arthritis) is the name for the typical wearing away of the cartilage on the bone surfaces to the point of damage. Eventually, there is bone on bone, and pain receptors are triggered. People with arthritis do not experience smooth movement of the joints, causing creaking or crepitus in those joints. This is the point in typical arthritis when it is tough to move the joint without discomfort. If the knee or hip joint is affected, walking becomes very difficult. When arthritis gets to the stage in which even pain or anti-inflammatory medications no longer help, then a surgeon might opt for a total joint replacement to restore function to the patient.

This is a typical scenario for most senior citizens. Arthritis happens. A joint cannot stay young forever. But it is interesting to see that individuals who have been consistent with exercises for years have remained ambulatory with minimal pain even late into their nineties. Hazel, who lived until the age of 103, walked briskly every day of her adult life. Other seniors, when walking had become difficult, switched to riding a stationary bike to keep their joints moving. Movement helps arthritis.

In the early stages of arthritis pain (let's say, age sixty) you may start to get a little "catch" or pain in the knee. You notice it most often after a long car ride or first thing in the morning. Instinctively, you start to favor that knee. You stop walking as long as you used to or not push it quite as hard as before in fear that there is something wrong with it. You think that some day you should get it checked. But you don't and you just live with it. Years go by and one of two things happened: either it cleared up on its own or the pain had made it difficult to walk. Sometimes joint pain does go away–primarily because of the way joint surfaces get nutrition. But cartilage, which is the lining surface of the joint as well as padding between the bones, has a poor blood supply. Because of this, it doesn't get fed its nutrients as do other tissues of the body that have a good blood supply, like muscles. Cartilage gets its nutrients from fluid (synovial fluid inside the joint) exchange. It is actual joint movement that allows the joint itself to become flexible and compression forces of the joint fluids to rebuild and repair itself. The process can be compared to working taffy. When taffy is cold and dormant, it is hard and brittle, but when you start to pull it or "exercise" it, it becomes moldable or pliable. The pain you first feel might cause you to not move the joint much for fear that something is wrong. But movement is usually precisely what the joint needs for a consistent length of time.

The other thing that could happen after initial knee pain is an ongoing progression of pain. If pain does not go away naturally, the joint cartilage itself could have been significantly damaged and in need of arthroscopic surgery by an orthopedic surgeon.

Or it could just be in need of disciplined exercise. Either way, once pain appears in the knee or any other joint due to normal arthritic changes, exercising the joint to replenish with nutrients should always be the first treatment choice. A good orthopedic surgeon will diagnose the difference between significant cartilage damage that requires surgery and joint pain that could be treated with exercise.

When arthritis becomes significant and there is much difficulty walking, use of a stationary bike will continue to ensure nutrient exchange to the joint, slowing the arthritic process without the painful weight-bearing of walking or running. Movement will help arthritis, especially in the early stages and also as a preventative measure before symptoms even start.

Exercise and osteoporosis: Without fail, exercise will help slow the progression of osteoporosis. The effects of weight-bearing exercises like walking or running cause an increase in the density of bone. The effectiveness is directly proportional to the intensity of the exercises. Weight lifting exercises will also help increase bone density. It has been shown to be as effective—if not more effective—than the use of prescription drugs for osteoporosis. But clinical trials highlight the value of using exercise in conjunction with the prescription medications for the battle against advancing osteoporosis.

The most effective prevention of osteoporosis is early rigorous exercise that includes weight-bearing and some sort of weight lifting (free weights, exercise bands, or weight machines). For women, exercise battles osteoporosis best if they are pre-menopausal, but post-menopausal women find benefit from exercise and osteoporosis prevention as well.

Exercise and heart disease: The heart and lungs are strengthened with exercise. Typically, aerobic type exercise (walking, running, bicycling) works best to improve the condition of the cardiovascular and respiratory systems (heart, lungs, blood vessels, and blood). Aerobic activity stimulates the oxygen exchange of all the organs and encourages healing in any part of the body. What is considered aerobic activity? An easy rule of thumb when you are exercising is, if you can talk in a short sentence without gasping, that is considered aerobic. If you can talk in long-sentence conversation without breathing heavily, the exercise level might not be challenging enough. Pick up the pace in order to get a maximum benefit of your aerobic efforts. If you gasp for breath at every word, you might be going too hard; slowing down in order to exercise for a longer time or distance would be more beneficial.

Destructive habits, like smoking, not only compromise breathing and make exercise difficult, but they can also negatively affect healing and increase pain following an injury. The more you improve your cardiovascular system through disciplined exercises and non-destructive habits, the better the rest of your body systems work because of the key role your heart and lungs have on bringing oxygenated blood to all parts of the body.

Exercise and hypertension: Hypertension or high blood pressure often can be managed with exercise. As you exercise over time, the heart becomes more efficient at pumping a larger volume of blood per beat. Since hypertension is excessive pressure against the walls of the blood vessels throughout the body, the more efficiently the heart pumps or forces blood out with each contraction, the less constant tension there will be on the blood vessel walls to move the same amount of blood.

Stress is also a risk factor for hypertension. The sympathetic nervous system is stimulated with stress. We have a heightened sensitivity in times of anxiety. This is helpful when we are in danger, but not when it is self-inflicted or the result of lifestyle choices. When we are stressed, blood flow is constricted to our digestive system to allow more blood for our muscular system—in case we need to fight or flee from danger. Among other things, stress causes an increase in blood pressure and heart rate. If stress is a way of life, one may be at risk for digestive problems, disturbed sleeping patterns, even stroke and heart attack. Long-term effects of disciplined exercise may decrease in the stress of daily life by improving the cardiac output as well as releasing natural chemicals that reduce anxiety.

Excessive body fat also puts more stress on the heart to pump. The less body fat one has, the less stress one has on the heart and blood vessels as they pump the same volume of blood through the body. So exercise not only reduces body fat, but it will directly decrease the tension on the heart and blood vessel walls, therefore moving blood more efficiently through the body. This, in turn, reduces hypertension.

Exercise and stroke: A stroke happens when part of the brain does not have rich oxygenated blood circulating to it. A stroke can be caused by a thrombosis in which plaque (fatty deposit) is built up inside the blood vessel and finally occludes or chokes off the blood to a particular part of the brain. It can also be caused by an embolism in which the blood vessel is blocked off from plaque that has formed elsewhere, broken free, and settled in the small blood vessels of the brain causing a blocking of the blood. Either way, that part of the brain will die. A third way a stroke happens is by a hemorrhage, in which a blood vessel in the brain bursts under pressure or at a weakened spot in the vessel wall causing blood to spill out of the vessel and kill the part of the brain that no longer gets blood delivered to it. In each case, the better the circulation, the more pliable the blood vessels, and the lower the blood pressure, the lower the risk of a stroke. Understand that consistent exercise contributes positively to all of these things. Exercise improves circulation, makes blood vessels more pliable by reducing the buildup of plaque, and lowers blood pressure. Therefore, consistent exercise, especially aerobic exercise, reduces the risk of stroke.

Exercise and diabetes: Diabetes is a condition that affects millions. There are two types of diabetes: Type I and Type II. Type I, formally called juvenile diabetes, is the direct result of the pancreas not producing insulin. Type I usually starts in childhood and may be present at birth, but most often is a result of an autoimmune reaction in which the pancreas is affected by a virus. In Type II diabetes, the pancreas produces too little insulin, or the body has built a resistance to insulin and it is not as effective in using glucose (sugar) for energy from the cells. Type II diabetes represents 90 percent of all diabetes and is the one that has grown to epidemic proportions in the United States. This epidemic has been linked directly to extremely poor diets and sedentary lifestyles.

The bottom line is the following regarding diabetes: damage is done to the body when sugar levels in the blood are too high or last too long. This can lead to cardiac conditions, blindness, kidney failure, stroke, or infection resulting in amputation. Exercise is a natural way to bring blood sugars down.

When you are at rest, your body (muscles and heart) demands only a little sugar (glucose) be used for energy. With exercise, the demand for sugar greatly increases in the muscles and blood-sugar levels come down if they were running high. A sedentary individual who never exercises, sometimes experiences blood-sugar levels that stay higher. When you add to this high-sugar condition an unhealthy diet of excessive carbohydrates like refined sugar and processed flour, the individual's blood-sugar will start to rise simply because the body becomes resistant to the excessive amounts of sugar in the blood. In other words, the insulin is no longer effective enough to keep up with all those excess carbohydrates and no other way to burn all that sugar in the blood. Exercise works incredibly well to counter this problem. As you increase the demand on the body, the blood-sugar levels come down. Healthy, exercised muscles have the capacity to rapidly select the fuel source they need, sugar or fat, during times of fasting or feeding.[7] Untrained muscles or unexercised muscles are more insulin resistant—unable to use sugar efficiently for energy even with insulin present. Think of unexercised muscles as having less ability to use the energy source they have. That is why the more you exercise the better you are at utilizing calories—and the less likely you are to develop Type II diabetes or obesity.

A word of caution regarding exercise for Type I diabetics or Type II diabetics who have a pancreas that is unable to produce enough insulin: vigorous exercise is so efficient at burning off excessive sugar that it is easy to go below your normal, healthy blood-sugar level and produce a low blood-sugar condition while you exercise. For this reason, it is most important to know your sugar levels if you've been diagnosed with diabetes. You need to stabilize your sugars by using the right amount of exercise along with the right dosage of insulin and the right amount of food, specifically carbohydrates.

This information should be a wake-up call for those who have very poor diets, who are obese, and don't exercise. It is this group that is most at risk for developing Type II diabetes. If they consistently exercise and eat healthy they will greatly reduce their risk by giving their pancreas a break from the diet it was never intended by nature to handle.

In addition to chronic conditions requiring medications, exercise addresses other aspects of aging in ways no other medication or activity can.

Exercise and posture and flexibility: Along with strength, flexibility is also compromised with a sedentary lifestyle. Just by adding activity to an inactive lifestyle, general flexibility will improve. But, specific muscle groups should be addressed as well. As we age, our posture typically changes, mostly due to the effects of gravity, sarcopenia, and osteoporosis. We develop rounded shoulders and a forward head posture due to loss of flexibility of the chest and neck muscles, while weakening the muscles that keep the spine and shoulder blades in an erect position. This causes the shoulders and neck to slump forward, changing the posture. Exercises, specifically strengthening exercises, can address these areas to make sure the postural muscles and the chest and neck muscles maintain their strength and flexibility.

Also, muscles of the hips and legs tend to lose flexibility with prolonged sitting or inactivity. It is important to maintain flexibility and strength of these areas to ensure correct posture and function. When you don't exercise, the muscles in the hips (hip flexors) become shortened because of excessive sitting. With exercise you get to use the muscles' full available range of motion. The same is true for the muscles in the back of the legs, the hamstrings. Sitting causes this group of muscles to shorten. Standing and exercising, allows these muscles to work through their full range of motion. Aerobic activity improves circulation and this also assists in giving the muscles back their normal flexibility.

Exercise and depression: Exercise also affects depression in a positive way. Addictive substances, such as alcohol, cocaine, and tobacco, stimulate the areas of the brain that cause a craving for *more;* so does exercise. Exercise, once a routine, becomes a healthy stimulant that can satisfy addictive cravings. Destructive addictive habits are replaced by exercise, the healthy alternative. Exercise stimulates endorphins which functions like an anti-depressant. So, the more you exercise, the more you desire to exercise and the less depressed you feel. Along with improved strength, endurance, flexibility, balance, and reduced risk of osteoporosis and sarcopenia, the benefit of reduced levels of depression is also a benefit with consistent exercise.

Exercise and health care: It is apparent that exercise has positive effects on almost all chronic conditions. Since many of these conditions are worsened with obesity and poor diet, a nation that exercises and eats healthier food, will spend less on health care. Remember those healthiest people in the world in Okinawa, Japan, and Sardinia, Italy? Their national health-care systems are not as generous as is the U. S. system, and very little is spent on prescription medications. A healthy, whole-food diet and daily exercise appear to make the difference.

Questions to Ponder
What is my understanding of the relationship between health and exercise? How can my exercising better reduce my health risks as I grow older?

Exercise and Metabolism

A closer look at the effects of exercise and diet can help us better understand their involvement in battling obesity. It is time to forget the breakthrough diet and self-help books, the new improved exercise programs and gadgets, the easy diet pill, and food discovery. What's true today has always been true: If you consistently take in more calories than you burn, you will eventually gain body fat. If you consistently burn more calories than you take in, you will eventually lose body fat. All permanent weight loss hangs on this principle. Success at any diet will boil down to that relationship. The caloric intake cannot exceed the calorie output. Simple physiology dictates that you will gain weight if input is greater than output, whether the calories are proteins, fats, or carbohydrates. Your body will either store calories away or burn them for energy.

More muscle, more calories: Weight loss through exercise is affected by overall muscle size. Quite simply, the more muscle you have, the easier it is to burn fat. Muscle burns calories and fat does not. Plain and simple, fat cannot burn calories. Fat is stored calories. Aerobic conditioning and weight lifting both will burn calories. The calories burned in an exercise routine are directly proportional to the amount of lean body mass or muscle that you have. The calorie is actually a measurement of heat. The bigger your engine, the more potential you have to make heat. Better put . . . the bigger the fireplace (muscle), the more wood (calories) you can burn at one time.

After weight lifting, your body uses extra calories to grow the muscle. Muscle growth (hypertrophy) utilizes extra calories following a workout. After a weight training session, micro-tears in the muscles happen. This is a normal occurrence. During the next couple of days, proteins help to repair and rebuild the muscles. This takes calories. Muscle hypertrophy or growth happens, and a bigger engine results.

As stated before, calories must come from a well-balanced diet. This is most important to remember when you are trying to build a bigger engine. Weight lifting and starvation will never work together. If you really want to lose body fat, create a bigger engine and burn more calories all day long.

Weight lifting—whether using dumbbells, exercise bands, or machines—is a vital component of the exercise program to maintain current muscle mass. If done correctly and with the right intensity, weight lifting can truly reverse the natural aging process by maintaining or even growing the muscles that tend to shrink (sarcopenia).

Slow and steady: If you lose weight too rapidly, you can lose muscle as well. When high physical demands are put on a body that is in a "starvation" mode, the body retrieves extra calories for energy from proteins (muscle) and other places as well as stored fat. This is why when you starve and exercise, you cannot expect optimum results. The effects of this can be seen with individuals who deny themselves food but also have an insatiable need to exercise excessively. This potentially dangerous combination may be diagnosed as anorexia nervosa. Since a young person's body needs energy for growing, it searches out any calories it can find to feed the obsession and can damage various systems of the body in the process.

If you average approximately 500 calories burned (used) daily with exercise, you will burn 3,500 calories extra each week with exercise. This means losing approximately one pound of fat per week, if calorie intake remains constant. One or two pounds a week of body fat lost is to be the safest and most permanent pace to lose weight.

Some people have a tendency to gain body fat more quickly than others, but it still holds true that it takes excess calories to create additional body fat. A tendency to gain body fat or a difficulty reducing body fat is often referred to as having a slow metabolism. A slow metabolism is often a result of low activity. A high metabolism is typically due to high activity. So metabolism usually reflects the number of calories that have been expended or burned in a day. Since food is input and exercise or activity is output, finding that balance between input and output is the key to weight maintenance.

The difference between someone who has an office job and someone who has a job involving physical labor could be the difference of 150 calories burned each working hour. If an average workday is eight hours, 1,200 extra calories are used each day. You can easily see how simple obesity can result from losing the balance between input and output.

A slow metabolism can be kick-started in a few different ways with exercise. When you exercise with intensity, your body has to rebuild everything that you've exhausted. Your body uses calories to replenish energy resources, perform minor muscular tissue repair, re-oxygenate blood, decrease body temperature, and return ventilation and heart rate to normal.[8] This accounts for extra calories burned following high-intensity exercise. These are calories over and above the initial calories spent while doing the exercise and are directly proportional to the intensity of the exercise. The number is higher in weight lifting than aerobic activity. If you were to exercise with intensity every day, your metabolism would actually increase. In other words, you would become more efficient at burning body fat through disciplined exercise.

Exercise and energy sources: The body uses its energy sources differently. The quickest and strongest muscle contractions use sugar as an energy source. Weight lifting burns plenty of sugar or glucose because of the short duration and explosive nature of the exercise. Intense weight lifting is performed without oxygen (anaerobic).

When beginning an exercise, muscles are powered almost exclusively by the immediate energy source, glucose. If exercise continues, the body will start demanding oxygen. If the exercise does not become too intense for regular breathing, oxygen can be supplied through the bloodstream and an aerobic exercise can continue.

During heavy weight lifting, the exercises are too demanding to supply oxygen to the muscle that is being worked. A burning sensation in the working muscle occurs when the muscle begins to fatigue. The burn is caused by lactic acid. This acid is a by-product of glucose burned without oxygen. This is a normal and necessary chemical reaction when weight lifting. For maximum results from weight lifting, it is important to feel the burn. Over the course of a workout, as sugar (glucose) becomes less readily available, a maximum muscle contraction becomes more difficult. Weight lifting is most efficient when sugar (glucose) is at its peak, that is, at the beginning of a workout routine.

The truth is, both sugar and fat are always feeding the muscles during aerobic activity, but their relationship is inversely proportional to each other. As glucose is used more and more in exercise, it eventually is less and less plentiful and fat plays a more active role in feeding the muscles during aerobic activity.

So, since sugar (glucose) starts strong at the beginning of exercise, fat will be used for energy in higher proportion when sugar is less available later in the same aerobic exercise session. Although fat is not metabolized for energy during weight lifting (or at least in much less proportion than sugar), it metabolizes nicely with plenty of oxygen and is a good aerobic energy source when glucose is low.

In order to perform an intense weight lifting program, sugar (glucose) availability should be at its highest level. Simply put, weights done prior to aerobic activity will best utilize your body's natural sugar (glucose) storage. Fat burns nicely with oxygen. So when it is time for the aerobic portion of your workout, you will be further along into your body's natural fat storages. Also, aerobic exercise assists in the removal of lactic acid that is built-up from weight lifting by flooding the muscles with fresh oxygenated blood. This reduces the potential for ongoing muscle soreness.

This concept of energy sources that the body uses is complicated, but helpful to understand. The physiological breakdown of how the muscles use their energy sources is an amazing phenomenon, but hard to visualize. It might be helpful to re-explain it with this analogy: Imagine you have two fuel tanks that your body can use for energy during exercise. These tanks contain sugar and fat. Your body always prefers to use sugar because it is quick, easy to use, and doesn't require you to supply it with oxygen (you don't even have to breathe to use it). Fat is a little more complicated. It requires work to "unpack it," transport it, and burn it with oxygen. Eventually fat will give you energy. The fat tank is used more as your sugar tank goes down, aerobically.

Now, you decide to start weight lifting. You go at it for twenty minutes. You used up a lot of your sugar tank and didn't even touch your fat tank. Why? Oh yeah, fat can burn only with oxygen. Remember that weight lifting is anaerobic or without oxygen because it is quick, intense, and explosive in nature.

Now it is time to jog, but you only have a limited amount of sugar left. You will never have the energy to finish a twenty-minute run that you had planned. Then it occurs to you, jogging is aerobic because you can breathe while you do it and that supplies the muscles with fresh oxygen through the bloodstream. You still have a full fat tank. Fat and sugar can both burn with oxygen. And, because you have used up a lot of your sugar during weight lifting, you will certainly burn more fat for energy than you would have if you only went for a jog. So go ahead, tap into the fat tank. It burns nicely with oxygen.

What happens if you decide to run first? Well, your body still prefers using sugar because it is so easy to use for energy. When you finish your run, you have much less sugar in your tank, but you still have a whole lot of fat left in its tank. You go to start your weight lifting. What happens? You have no strength left. Then you remember; fat cannot burn without oxygen. Weight lifting is anaerobic so it needs lots of sugar (glucose). You have a tank full of fat and no way to tap it because there is no oxygen. This weight lifting session was not as beneficial as it could have been. Not only did you get stronger muscle contractions by doing weight lifting first, but also you burned much more fat during your jog simply due to the order of the exercise.

Clearly, doing weight training (anaerobic exercise) first gives you the best fat-burning results. But, remember that much more important than the order of exercise is the fact that you do any exercise. And remember to start any exercise with a light warm-up.

Truly, any exercise is better than no exercise. Doing exercise you enjoy will ensure long-term, disciplined commitment. The long-term benefits of exercise far outweigh any short-term effects that we might set as goals, such as losing fifteen pounds in six weeks. It is the long term benefits of disciplined exercise that will create a healthier body and a more efficient metabolism. Exercise that includes both aerobic and weight-lifting components will guarantee a better metabolism that burns calories more efficiently and with less effort. It will battle the effects of sarcopenia, osteoporosis, obesity, postural changes, and other physical problems that come with aging. A key to improving metabolism is a disciplined exercise routine.

Questions to Ponder

How can I more effectively choose exercises and manage my metabolism? How will a more efficient metabolism, lower body fat, increased strength and flexibility, and fewer health problems with aging affect my ability to serve?

Exercise for Peace

Exercise is more than just another activity that needs to be done each day. Scheduled demands mean that you wake up, shower, eat breakfast, work, eat lunch, work more, eat supper, spend time with the kids and spouse, maybe watch television, then sleep again. Somewhere among the scheduled demands there needs to be time for exercise.

Integrated exercise: Exercise is not another commitment to be penciled into an already busy agenda. Exercise is a lifestyle change. It is looking at your life differently. Instead of seeing the day as a series of to-do activities in which exercise is just another activity, exercise should just be part of an overall healthier lifestyle.

Integrating exercise in a healthy lifestyle might mean your lunch break is twenty minutes on a treadmill and a fruit salad. It might entail a run in the morning before a shower as meditation time with God. It might be walking with a significant other. As you work off the frustrations of the day with exercise, you and your spouse, friend, or exercise partner are accountable to and supportive of each other in your fitness plans. Exercise could also be integrated into what happens at church—exercise with prayer or with a study group that creatively ties wellness with devotions.

Exercise is a lifestyle change that is addictive—in a good way—if it is done consistently and as a priority. Before long, you will find that all other things will fall into place. You will see that you're changing your eating habits because you become acutely aware of empty calories, and you begin to feel compassion for those who go without food. Your friends, children, and community see you, and in turn, they may become inspired by your efforts, so they join the cause. Expect to excite others with the healthy habits that you decided to adopt. Those who see you as a model of improved health will be strengthened by your determination and inspired to stop abusive behaviors. Most importantly, your family will follow your lead and live happier and healthier lives because you decided to care for yourself so you could better care for them.

Create a lifestyle that allows the space and time for healthy living. Do the following, if you are able. Climb stairs instead of using elevators, park in the back of parking lots, get on the floor with children, walk everywhere you can, bicycle more, drive less, dance, and turn off the television. Give thanks and be contented.

Exercise and nature: Strive for peace in your life. It is needed now more than ever. When it is time to vacation, consider the wilderness. The hiking trails, camps, canoeing, or other outdoor activities often create a closer connection to God and community. The many summers I took church groups to hike the Appalachian Trail are the closest experiences I have had to the fellowship of the first

Christians that we read about in the book of Acts. Those week-long events, combined with the fellowship, devotion, physical challenges, support, and overall goodwill of a Christian community surely parallels what the original Christians experienced when they gathered together.

In addition to the physical support each member of the hiking community gives to ensure everyone gets safely over and through the rocks and creeks, the community supports each other with its use of food rations. The stronger and more able hikers carry more weight than those who cannot. Skilled individuals support the community with their knowledge of fire building, cooking, and trail safety. All are cared for as needed. Every member has a part. Every member is vital to the health and safety of the community.

The culture of the hiking community in the national parks, the Appalachian Trail, and others national trails is to "leave no trace." It is the ecological responsibility of the individual to keep the natural resources intact for the wildlife, future visitors, and the larger global community. "Leave no trace" can be adapted to the Christian life and our interaction with our God-given resources. Being a good steward of our land will leave these resources for future generations.

Nature offers simplicity. When you are hiking, it is just you and the sounds of creation. Without cell phones, computers, televisions, and even automobiles, life is more simply lived and with greater clarity. Through nature, it is easier to get back in touch with our community, ourselves, and God. Our relationship with God is too often overshadowed by our "stuff." Get out into the woods, explore God's playground, and feel how easy it is to reconnect. Rediscover just how little we actually need to live fully. Everything needed to sustain life for days on end comes from a thirty-five-pound pack, a good pair of boots, community support, and fresh streams along the footpath.

When I think of being out in the elements, I am always reminded of the story of Elijah in the Old Testament. Elijah was a prophet who ran away to the mountains and away from the pressures and dangers of the world. Specifically, he was fleeing from the evil king Ahab and his queen Jezebel in fear of his life. God told him to stand at the opening of a cave in the mountains and wait for God to "pass by." As Elijah stood at the mouth of the cave, there was an earthquake, but God was not in it. A tremendous wind blew through, like a hurricane with enough wind to smash rocks, but God wasn't in that. Then a fire appeared, but God wasn't in that either. All of this chaos was followed by silence . . . and God was there. Elijah listened and understood.

When you reach the top of a mountain that you spent the last hour hiking up, you might not hear birds, insects, wind, or any sound at all at first. Then God will speak. By removing all the distractions and listening to the silence, you will find yourself in communion with the Creator. On the mountain or in the woods or on the ocean, when the noise is gone, God's voice is heard clearly. You may actually come down from the mountain redirected and remembering for what purpose you were created.

Christian discipleship and exercise: If fitness is your only goal, studies show that 50 percent of the time you will fail, within three to six months, to achieve it. Permanent weight loss is likely to fail by any method other than proper diet and exercise. With them, permanent weight loss is not only achieved, but maintained. Therefore, you need motivation for life. Fitness, injury prevention, and good health practices work together to improve your ability to care for your loved ones and faithfully carry out your life's mission. Be contented. Discover the freedom and fulfillment that the contented seniors have through serving a higher purpose in Christian discipleship. Change your focus to love.

Love changes the very essence of what life is all about. A goal that seemed out of reach is within reach, once the mindset is changed. Love is more satisfying than food or material possessions, and as a goal, it is more motivating and permanent than aesthetics or appearance. The contented seniors have given us the elements of a successful, disciplined, disability-free, weight-controlled, long life. Through love, fitness is achieved. Through compassion, the hungry will be fed.

There is a great irony in it all. The things we worry so much about, the things we think are so important—like amassing wealth—carry little weight at the end of the journey. The only thing that consistently mattered to the contented seniors, even through adversity, was love—the love they gave and the love they felt, and the difference they made for the better. The ultimately most valuable use of time is to extend yourself for the growth of others; that is, to spread love. Love provides the discipline that keeps us in healthy habits of diet and exercise for long life as Christian disciples. And finally, because of our loving choices and healthy changes, we can bring life to those who otherwise would starve.

Questions to Ponder
How important is peace in my life, and where do I experience it? What will I need to do differently to schedule thirty-to-sixty minutes of exercise into my day from now on?

Exercise
Ongoing disciplined exercise will reduce or reverse the aging process.

Exercise benefits: Regular exercise slows the natural aging process in many ways: reversing osteoporosis and muscle atrophy (sarcopenia); slowing formation of arthritis; decreasing body fat; improving posture, the immune system, and short-term memory; increasing cardiovascular output, lowering the risk of many cancers and diabetes; regulating sleep patterns, muscle balance, and coordination; enriching relaxation: decreasing hypertension, depression, anxiety, and stress; and improves self-image. Exercise is also linked to protecting against Alzheimer's disease.

Church gatherings: Your church's fellowship focus can be expanded. In addition to gathering around meals, gather in healthy alternatives like exercise classes or health-related workshops. Exercise components (simple stretching, walking, running, bicycling, use of exercise bands, or other athletic endeavors) could be added to Bible studies or prayer groups. Also, creating more outdoor ministry events that incorporate hiking, canoeing and other adventures, can reconnect us to creation and build a deeper appreciation and respect for our natural resources.

Simple changes: Parking in the back of parking lots or taking stairs instead of elevators will free up space for those who cannot get around as freely and add to your daily exercise. Bicycle to work or church. Turn off the television. Avoid excessive sitting. Replacing the computer chair with a therapy ball (75 cm) will greatly improve posture, as well as abdominal and trunk strength. Be creative—the more you move the better your health.

With thirty-to-sixty minutes of consistent exercise each day, you can burn an extra 500 calories daily. This may add up to almost a pound of body-fat a week—about fifty pounds of body-fat a year. Consistency in a lifestyle of exercise and healthy eating makes the difference. That is the way to health and weight-loss. Nothing else will substitute.

Chapter 4: Fit to Serve

The Well Church

> I give you a new commandment, that you love one another.
> —John 13:34

Fear has become a way of life. We are less and less likely to trust our neighbors. The environment is run as if it is going out of business. Instead of reaching out to those in need, we have built walls in fear. Fear has left the hands and feet of the "body of Christ" crippled.

Jesus was very deliberate about pointing out that the poorest and lowest of people are most deserving, and we should be humbled into service for their sake. The social action of loving each other, especially those who are needy, is what Jesus emphasizes should dictate our efforts and actions. He mentions the following: The last shall be first (Matthew 19:30), blessed are the poor in spirit, for theirs is the kingdom of heaven (Matthew 5:3), blessed are the meek, for they will inherit the earth (Matthew 5:5), and just as you did it to the least of these who are members of my family, you've done it unto me (Matthew 25:40). Countless other strong messages about social justice from Jesus appear throughout the Gospels, yet many of the topics we focus on as a church do not involve issues that Jesus directly addressed.

With profound hope, Christ calls us to care for others. When we feel that the world is doomed, Christ calls us to not worry about tomorrow (Matthew 6:25). We are to take a step back, reevaluate all things without fear, and then go forth to make things better for all people, because all of us were created in God's image, not just a privileged few. When in fear of our neighbors, Christ calls us to love them (Matthew 5:43). When food is scarce, Christ asks us to discover new and creative ways to feed everyone. To give to the poor is to be perfect (Matthew 19:21). When we invite the poor, crippled, lame, and blind (Luke 14:13), we are blessed by doing it, because those individuals cannot give anything in return.

For the individuals who enter the church for meaning and leave unsatisfied, the largest stumbling block is often this point of loving our neighbor. The unbelieving world sees the church as hypocritical when it confronts this altruistic command. They see us (the church) gathered together professing with our lips, but living like nothing is different. They feel the love of Christ is not as life-changing and revolutionary as we claim it is. They see us heatedly squabbling over issues and theological differences among our denominations, while millions are dying because they don't have the basics to sustain life. They see us spend fortunes on bricks and mortar, as brothers and sisters starve. They believe we are more interested in our own immediate needs, not the needs of our planet which God created wonderfully and without waste—except what we waste. They see us not seeming to be bothered much by our compromises, our excuses, and our failures.

In the New Testament alone, the word *love* is mentioned seventy-four times as well as many references to love and our neighbors are defined as everyone. We are told to care for the poor dozens of times over, and yet the church often appears to concentrate on tasks that just don't seem as important to Christ. And now faith, hope, and love abide, these three; and the greatest of these is love (1 Corinthians 13:13).

Jesus made it clear that a new commandment—love one another (John 13:34)—transcends all other commandments. Love is the action that distinguishes his followers (John 13:35). As easy as loving sounds, this new commandment is demanding. Love, Jesus-style, can not be done halfway. Whoever says, "I am in the light," while hating a brother or sister, is still in the darkness (1 John 2:9). "Love your neighbor as yourself" (Matthew 19:19). Believers may disagree on certain controversial issues, but one thing is and always has been a constant: we are to care for the poor. The command is repeated throughout the Bible and is rarely disputed among denominations.

Other religions share this concern for the poor. Islam, Judaism, Buddhism, and Hinduism all echo this understanding with Christians: we are to care for those who are poor, sick, old, disabled, and any others who cannot care for themselves.

The Qur'an, the Muslim Holy Scriptures, says the following: Righteousness is this: that one should . . . give away wealth out of love for him to the near of kin and the orphans and the needy and the wayfarer and the beggars and for the emancipation of the captives (2.177). The Old Testament prophets warn early Jews against neglecting the orphans, the poor, and the forgotten. Buddha said,

"If you do not tend to one another, then who is there to tend to you? Whoever would tend me, he should tend the sick" (Vinaya, Mahavagga 8:26.3). And of course Jesus' command to love one another throughout the New Testament is very clear.

Truly, it is part of God's plan to put aside differences of doctrine and dogma and work for humanity to support life through wellness for the human race. For us who claim Christ as our Lord and Savior, this can be done in community with all creeds and religions. Such cooperation will only enhance our understanding of how God is revealed to us personally through Jesus Christ. By embracing our brothers and sisters in community through love, all things are possible. Wars end, hungry mouths are fed, health improves, populations stabilize, the earth restores its resources and a deeper understanding of God's love exists for everyone.

Christian growth has been most dramatic, not as the result of wars, but following surges of good will. Early Christians became the counterculture of the Roman Empire. As we read about earlier, the first Christians and the first churches were communities that grew at light speed. What was the reason for the growth? When Rome threatened the Christian movement, many believers quietly continued to care for the poor, sick, and widowed. People of Rome began to take notice. Christians were martyred (killed for their cause), but that did not seem to stop the movement. Before long, a Jesus revolution took place, not by force or crusades, but by the exact opposite: love and compassionate works. The purity of doing good is universally understood. It supersedes force. Nonviolent compassionate works historically speak louder than war. Kingdoms rise and kingdoms fall, but love never dies. The word of the Lord endures forever (1 Peter 1:25).

We have seen beautiful examples of this love throughout the twentieth century. Communities stand together in acts of justice and peace and rise above the false strength of political might—ending apartheid in South Africa, desegregating of America's south, gaining India's independence, and Poland becoming a democracy are all real stories of what communities in action can accomplish with compassion and peace. Maybe the church is ready for another revolution, not by force, but by the opposite: compassion. If we were to love unconditionally by helping those who need it most, the world would take notice.

Our churches could raise awareness by becoming better stewards of our planet. Through the healthy lifestyle changes we Christians make, the church would encourage others to cherish our planet's resources. Through recycling, conservation, and simplifying, we could teach an easier way to a stable environment. Coffees we drink would be fair-traded coffees. The foods served at church functions would be with a deliberate support for local farmers who are not only fairly compensated for their efforts by the church, they would also be rewarded for doing the right thing for the earth (relying less on harmful pesticides and manufactured fertilizers, and relying more on crop rotations, manure fertilizers, diversified crops, and organic insecticides and pesticides). We would seek out and support more local growers who have struggled to stay in business with their crops and learn more about the food harvest seasons to better use foods when they are available and reduce waste. By supporting more local farmers, we would cut down on the fossil fuels being used to truck foods around from place to place, factory to factory. Eating more whole foods and less processed is healthier and generates less package waste than a diet of mostly processed foods. This is food as God intended for us to eat.

All this support would be done through churches, not by strong protest, but as a gentle encouragement to those companies and food co-ops that have always struggled to do the right thing for their patrons, employees, and environment. We would, as the first Christian community did, support each other in community so that no one, globally, would be forgotten. Through this quiet, peaceful support the church will sound a loud and powerful message about social justice, concern for our planet, and our desire to remain faithful stewards of all the resources that we have been so blessed with. When we support corporations that care for the planet and the worker, world markets will take notice. Companies will respond accordingly and make environmental and human rights as important as quarterly profits.

It is important that this silent support of socially concerned companies not be seen as a political statement or scheme. True compassion transcends politics. It is through love of each other in community and our God-given resources that we improve our health, our neighbor's health, and the wellness of our planet. We care for ourselves to better care for others.

If church members made the shift from the need-to-lose-weight paradigm to the need-to-feed-others paradigm, health costs would stabilize. Heart disease, stroke, hypertension, obesity, osteoporosis, arthritis, sarcopenia, and Type II diabetes would be the exception, no longer the norm. Also, longer, healthier lives would be more productive lives, allowing more active participation in social ministries. Older adults would be able to continue serving to the best of their physical abilities much later in life.

Food would be more evenly distributed throughout the world, and we would no longer spend the billions we currently spend on diet aids. We would eat healthier, while those who have nothing would be fed.

If we were to reduce our current diets of cheap meats, refined sugars, and processed flours and replace them with whole grains, beans, nuts, fruits, and vegetables, there would be increased volumes of more nutritious foods available to the world—including us. If, instead of the current American diet of predominantly animal-based foods, we would shift to predominantly plant-based foods, we would restore a balance in our personal and environmental health.

Churches can set the pace by designing group meals, potlucks, and celebrations to include healthy foods in modest amounts—with the additional goal of raising awareness of those who go without food. Churches could offer support groups and exercise classes that would encourage a lifetime of physical and spiritual renewal. Prayer for health and wellness would accompany our efforts to stay disability-free through disciplined exercise and healthy eating.

If churches encouraged more outdoor ministries, congregations would quickly learn to do more with less and with fewer distractions, like television and cell phones.

We would relearn to fully engage in each other in face-to-face communication while relying more on God's creation and less on our devices. Passion for environmental protection would soon be manifested around the community. A greater awareness of our natural resources would be instilled, not because it sounds like a good thing to protect, but because the community experiences it firsthand and realizes the tremendous loss that would happen if we continued to run our world's natural resources the way we are currently. Through compassion we could quietly protest against those establishments that disregard issues of ecology. Our purchases could support those companies that have struggled to do the right thing for people and the planet. Our investments in companies would no longer be determined based only on their quarterly returns, but also on the companies' policies of human rights, dignity to employees, and the way they treat the environment. Before long, other companies would take notice of the shift of critical analysis taken by investors, and they would be further inspired to do the right thing for the planet, their employees, and the investors.

Every church community is capable of starting their own wellness groups. Be creative in your churches and communities, and then share with everyone what you are doing. The motivation is contagious. For years now, I have lectured in churches that have started exercise classes, Tae Kwon Do classes, and nutrition and exercise support groups. Also, many churches have embraced the Fair Trade coffees, chocolates, teas, and cocoa sales for their members, food cooperatives with local farmers, migrant worker human rights advocacy and support groups, organic gardening classes, bike clubs, church landscaping using native plants for water conservation, outdoor ministry nature and wellness retreats, and car pooling for fuel conservation. All of these are missions with the common purpose of striving to be better stewards by improving personal health, and caring for others by protecting our resources.

Our very worship could even be influenced. Attending a worship service of a different religion can be an awakening experience. While I was in seminary, I went to a Muslim mosque. The Imam (the Muslim congregation's worship leader) was in his early seventies; I was in my mid-thirties. The service was approximately thirty minutes long. We assumed the multi-point positions always facing toward Mecca, the most holy place for Muslims. The positions were a series of bows, kneels, squats, reaches, and prayer stretches. This was done a total of seven times during the thirty minutes. By the end of the half hour, I found myself fatigued just by this prayer practice. It is one of the core beliefs of the Islamic religion that all Muslims pray this way five times every day. The Imam outdid me physically that day, even though he was twice my age. He was fit for the very physical worship that all Muslims do everyday, five times. As I prayed to Jesus throughout the service, I could not help but notice the pains I felt in my knees and back and the sweat that was dripping from my forehead.

In a Buddhist temple, I sat facing the temple worship leader who was in her early sixties. I was in my thirties. After twenty minutes in a cross-legged position on the floor, my knees, hips, and back hurt enough to interrupt my deep meditation on Christ. At the end of meditation, I noticed our worship leader jumped up from a cross-legged position while the rest of us, not conditioned for this physical challenge in their typical worship experience, slowly stood with discomfort.

Worship at a Hindu temple combined yoga meditation and positioning throughout the entire prayer-meditation session. We who were unaccustomed to this style of worship, had the hardest time with pain and concentration because of our personal deconditioned state.

Quite possibly, engaging the physical body in prayer, meditation, and worship, as other world religions do, improves physical fitness and deepens our focus on God. The Bible speaks of various positions of prayer: standing (Mark 11:25), lifting hands (Timothy 2:8), sitting (2 Samuel 7:18), kneeling (Luke 22:41; Acts 7:60, 9:40, 20:36, 21:5; Ephesians 3:14; 2 Chronicles 6:13; Daniel 6:10), looking upward (John 17:1), bowing down (Exodus 34:8), placing head between the knees (1 Kings 18:42), and falling on face prostrate to the Lord (Matthew 26:39, Mark 14:35). All positions are legitimate and might allow us to experience a deeper level of meditation and prayer, while fully engaging our physical bodies.

A deconditioned body tends to focus on aches, pains, restlessness, and fatigue and has more difficulty reaching deeper levels of communion with Christ. Healthy eating and exercises might assist your communion with Jesus by deepening your ability to meditate and pray without those aches, pains, restlessness, and fatigue.

Questions to Ponder

What tools does the church have to model, guide, and support members' choices for good? How can a church community be a wellness community?

The Individual

By the time you read this, my grandfather will have died. But, during the time of this writing, he lived with me.[1] My grandfather became a resident of my home in his ninety-third year. His mind was still good. He could remember most of the things he had done, and the things he had left undone. While I wrote, he lay in the hospital bed that my family had set up for him in our living room. He no longer had the ability to do anything on his own, but he did reflect.

My grandfather, Pappy, was a strong man. He was a man who moved furniture for a living. Pappy retired at age sixty-five and decided to quit the physical life. Like many of his generation, retirement meant staying at home, watching television, eating meals out, attending church and church picnics, and very little else. Pappy lived a physical life, but then he stopped. Almost thirty years later, he was unable to function. Arthritis had crippled his knees and hips. Sarcopenia had weakened his limbs and affected his ability to stand or pull himself to a standing position. His heart weakened, and he gained body fat from inactivity and a poor diet.

He had started to show signs of swelling in his legs from the weakened heart, skin discoloration from poor circulation, and chronic fatigue which left him sleeping the better part of the day. He was lucky to have lived as long as he did. Ninety-three is a ripe old age by any standard. Unfortunately, he had become prematurely disabled due to the accumulative affects of aging. Chances are that he could have been disability-free even in his ninety-third year if he had been disciplined with healthy habits and exercise following his retirement.

His last days were full of wonderful memories of days gone by. His stories were rich and focused on those simpler times in which he was fully alive, serving his family on the farm with his eleven brothers and sisters. Fond memories of his church and his civic club were among his shared stories. His peace came from the Scriptures. Until just a few weeks before the time of this writing, he was able to open his Bible on his own. Now he is unable, and I became his reader. The following was one of our favorites:

> For I am convinced that neither death, nor life, nor angels, nor rulers, nor things present, nor things to come, nor powers, nor height, nor depth, nor anything else in all creation, will be able to separate us from the love of God in Christ Jesus our Lord.
> —Romans 8:38-39

In the end, it was his reflection of the promise of Christ's love that gave him comfort. Without the love he felt, life in the end would have not made sense at all. In fact, it would have all been a tragic mistake, a pitiful existence, a selfish act of meaningless events. But, as for so many contented elderly, love built the bridge between his struggles and his understanding. Love was the catalyst for his meaningful existence. Pappy, like thousands of seniors I have worked with, ended their lives content in the promise, the promise of a new creation in Christ.

It is only by God's grace that we are made whole. God's love and commitment is revealed to us through the vulnerability of the cross. Our striving for personal health and wellness is incomplete without remembering the promise we have been given by God through faith in Christ. With Jesus, we die to the old and are made a new creation. Our poor health and destructive habits are given up at the foot of the cross, and our lives are made new through the resurrection. Thanks be to God.

As new creations in Christ, we have ears to hear. This opens the door to answer the health problems for both of the global extremes of overabundance and scarcity. When we are disciplined with our overabundance while concerning ourselves with the poor, a redistribution of resources occurs throughout the global community. We eat smarter. We purchase foods more carefully. We are concerned with the treatment of our natural resources. We support local farmers. We concern ourselves with poverty. We stay disciplined in exercise. We avoid unhealthy habits. We become better stewards of our bodies. This is compassionate wellness.

In this new paradigm shift, wellness is no longer self-centered, but centered on Christ and the least of these, our neighbors. Such a shift is permanent, and all-encompassing. We are to care for ourselves to better care for others. Aging health problems, obesity, and world hunger can be cured with compassion.

Love one another. Your global community is counting on you to do just that.

Peace.

Questions to Ponder
How am I better able to fulfill Jesus' command
to care for those in need if I am well and at peace?
What concrete steps will I take to change my own
personal health, improve the health of my faith
community, and care for the global community?

Fit to Serve
Every dollar spent, every action, and yes, even every
meal eaten, ultimately works for or against the health
of every person in our global community. If we follow
Christ's directive to show compassion to our neighbors,
we also will find the greatest way to health. Obesity and
world hunger both can be cured with compassion.

Summary

Buy Consciously

By considering every purchase (especially food) in terms of how it affects the global community and not just our wallets, we create a new reality. Supporting the Third World through creative and fair economic principles—such as environmentally conscious eating, recycling, investing in responsible foreign and domestic companies, and purchasing organic, Fair Trade coffees and other commodities from shops like Ten-Thousand Villages or other faith-based efforts—will give economic resources to those who had none before.

Control Population Explosions

When young women who never had life alternatives are offered a means to make a living, they are allowed to create a livelihood for themselves and their families. Such opportunities prove time and time again to reduce the birthrate per family, improve the health and well being of each child born, and promise a brighter future for the next generation. Opportunity, not poverty, is the only sane and positive way to stabilize world population explosions.

Change the World through Diet and Exercise

When you decide to consciously shift your eating and exercise toward thinking of the global community, you can reduce your garbage by about a thousand pounds a year, single-handedly. In the process, you could greatly reduce your potential dependency on national health-care. You could support those who are poor through your purchases. You could help to stabilize overpopulation in the Third World. You could directly improve care for the environment—while you maintain your own healthy body weight. You could help to reduce dependency on fossil fuels and promote the conservation of our precious life-giving water. Now imagine if you encouraged your local church or community, say one hundred people, to do the same. Then, they did the same until all were caring for themselves to better care for others. The world would have gone though a revolutionary paradigm shift that started as a spark in a local church by an individual.

Notes

Introduction

1. Thoreau, Henry David, *Walden and Other Writings* (New York: Bantam Books, 1962), 8.

Chapter 1: The Way

1. DeSilva, David, *An Introduction to the New Testament, Contexts, Methods and Ministry Formation* (Downers Grove, Ill.: Intervarsity Press, 2004), 208.
2. Sobrino, Jon, *Jesus the Liberator* (Maryknoll, New York: Orbis Books, 2003).
3. "The Way" is one of the original terms that defined the Christian movement through the first century C.E. or A.D. "Christian" was not used until late in the first century and was first used by the people of Antioch. The Way was used mostly to describe this "new way" of treating each other as a Nazarene named Jesus taught us to treat each other . . . the original Christian community. Other original names were "the believers" and "the sect of the Nazarenes."
4. Battle, Michael, "How Do We Live?" Cited in *Essentials of Christian Theology* (Peabody, Mass.: Westminster John Knox Press, 2003), 291.
5. Aikman, David, *Great Souls: Six Who Changed the Century* (Nashville: Word Publishing, 1998), 122-23.
6. Ackerman, Peter and Jack Duvall, *A Force More Powerful: A Century of Nonviolent Conflict* (New York: Palgrave, 2000), 66-67.

7. Bonhoeffer, Dietrich, *Life Together* (New York: HarperCollins Publishers, 1954), 21.
8. Putnam, Robert D., *Bowling Alone* (New York: Simon and Schuster, 2000).
9. Peck, M. Scott, *The Different Drum* (New York: Simon and Schuster, 1987), 86-106.
10. Zizza C., Siega-Riz AM, Popkin BM. Significant increase in young adults' snacking between 1977-1978 and 1994-1996 represents a cause for concern! *Preventive Medicine* 2001; 32:303. Bower, Del. "Cooking trends echo changing roles of women." *Food Review* 2000:23 (I):23-29. Cited from *Food Politics*, Nestle, Marion (Berkley and Los Angeles: University of California, 2002), 19.
11. Peck, M. Scott, *The Road Less Traveled* (New York: Simon and Schuster, 1978), 81.
12. The origin of this story is unknown. It could possibly be folklore although it seems to encapsulate the compassionate ministry of Mother Teresa.
13. Koenig, Harold, M.D., *The Healing Power of Faith* (Simon and Schuster, New York, 1999), 24.
14. Kolata, Gina, *Ultimate Fitness: The Quest for Truth about Exercise and Health* (New York: Farrar, Straus, and Giroux, 2003), 195.
15. Bartholomew, J., David Morrison, and Joseph Ciccolo. "Effects of Acute Exercise on Mood and Well Being in Patients with Major Depressive Disorder," *Medicine and Science in Sports and Exercise*, Vol. 37, no. 12, Dec. 2005, 2032-37.
16. Covey, Stephen, *The 7 Habits of Highly Effective People* (New York: Simon and Schuster, 1989), 305.
17. Shaw, George Bernard (1856-1950), cited from Covey, 299.
18. Frankl, Viktor, *Man's Search for Meaning* (New York: Simon and Schuster, 1959), 48-49.

Chapter 2: Food

1. Fuhrman M.D., Joel, *Eat to Live* (New York: Time Warner, 2003).
2. Food, Field Reporter, March 20, 1939. Cited from *Paradox of Plenty,* 21.
3. U.S. Congressional Research Service, "The Role of the Federal Government in Human Nutrition Research" (Washington, D.C.: USGPO, 1976), 116. Cited from *Paradox of Plenty,* 74.
4. *Time,* Dec. 7, 1959. Cited from *Paradox of Plenty,* 115.
5. Nestle, Marion, *Food Politics* (Berkeley and Los Angeles: University of California Press, 2003), 11.
6. Ibid., 11.
7. Ibid., 8.
8. http://www.vegetarian-nutrition.info/nuggets/child_obesity.php.
9. *New York Times,* April 25, 1961. Cited from *Paradox of Plenty,* 167.
10. Nestle, Marion, *Food Politics,* 283. In cases like the ephedrine-containing supplements for weight loss, the FDA reported more than eight hundred cases of side-effects and twenty to thirty deaths between 1993 and 1997. Even so, in 1999, just *one* top selling ephedrine-containing supplement generated sales of $900 million. Finally, in 2003, the FDA recommended a ban on the sale of these products. Even with the strong warnings, they are still available and continue to be marketed.
11. Sachs, Jeffery, *The End of Poverty* (London: Penguin Books, 2006), 1.
12. Kushner, Harold, *Living a Life That Matters* (New York: Random House, 2001), 83.
13. Robbins, J., and A. Mortifee, *In Search of Balance* (Tiburon, Calif.: H. J. Kramer, 1991), 96-97.
14. Willcox, Willcox, and Suzuki, *The Okinawa Program* (New York: Clarkson Potter/Publications).

15. Ibid., 71.
16. Buettner, Dan, "New Wrinkles on Aging," *National Geographic* (November 2005, vol. 208), 5.
17. Levenstein, Harvey, *Paradox of Plenty: A Social History of Eating in Modern America* (Berkeley and Los Angeles: University of California Press), 66.
18. Dr. David Jenkins, Toronto, Canada, had started the work on the Glycemic Index in 1981. In many studies, white bread is used as the standard of measure at 100.
19. Nestle, Marion, *Food Politics,* vii.
20. *Gandhi.* Director Richard Attenborough. With Ben Kingsley and Candice Bergen. Columbia Pictures, 1982.
21. Rolls, Barbara and Robert Barnett, *The Volumetrics: Weight-Control Plan* (New York: Harper Torch, 2003).
22. Fuhrman, 7.
23. Batmanghelidj, F., *Water for Health, for Healing, for Life* (New York: Warner Books, 2003), 32-34.
24. Thoreau, Henry David, *Walden and Other Writings* (New York: McGraw-Hill, 1988), 13.
25. O'Brien P., "Dietary Shifts and Implications for U. S. Agriculture." *American Journal of Clinical Nutrition* 1995:61 (suppl.): 1390s-1396s. Young CE, Kantor LS. "Moving Toward the Food Guide Pyramid: Implications for U. S. Agriculture." (Washington, D.C.: USDA, 1999), cited in Nestle, M. *Food Politics,* 363.
26. Kelly Brownell, Yale Center for Eating and Weight Disorders, cited from *SuperSize Me,* Directed by Morgan Spurlock (New York: Hart Sharp Video), 2004.
27. Brownell, K., *Food Fight* (New York: McGraw-Hill, 2004), 3.
28. Ibid., 46.
29. Tremblay, Mark S., et al. "Conquering Childhood Inactivity: Is the Answer in the Past?" *Medicine & Science in Sports & Exercise,* vol. 37, no. 7, July 2005.
30. Louv, Richard, *Last Child in the Woods: Saving Our Children from Nature Deficit Disorder* (New York: Workman Publishing, 2005).

31. Spurlock, Morgan. *Supersize Me.* Directed by Morgan Spurlock (New York: Hart Sharp Video), 2004.

32. Reyte, Elizabeth, *Garbage Land: On the Secret Trail of Trash* (New York: Little, Brown and Company, 2005), 283.

33. Hepperly, P., et al., "Environmental, Energetic, and Economic Comparisons of Organic and Conventional Farming Systems," *BioScience,* July 2005, vol. 55, no. 7.

34. Interview with Paul Hepperly in July of 2005 at the Rodale Institute.

35. Taken from the ECHO Web site (www.echonet.org).

36. Meadows, Donella, "Our Food, Our Future," *Organic Gardening* (www.organicgardening.com/featureprint/1,7759,sl-5-20-908,00.html).

37. Robbins, John, *May All Be Fed: Diet for a New World* (New York: William Morrow and Company, Inc., 1992), 35.

38. Ibid., 34.

39. Ibid., 35.

40. Cohen, Ben and Jerry Greenfield, *Ben & Jerry's Double Dip* (New York: Simon and Schuster, 1997). 30.

41. Levenstein, Harvey *Paradox of Plenty: A Social History of Eating in Modern America* (Berkeley and Los Angeles: University of California Press, 2003), 145. Taken from U. S. Senate, Select Committee on Nutrition and Human Needs, Nutrition and Health 2: committee print, 94th Congress, 2nd Session, 1976, 56; *New York Times,* June 6, 1963; Irene Wolgamot, "The World Food Congress," JHE 55 (August 1963), 603.

42. Robbins, 35.

43. Sachs, Jeffrey D., *The End of Poverty* (London: Penguin Books, 2006), 324.

44. Ibid., 325.

45. Ibid., 326.

46. Rogers, Heather, *Gone Tomorrow: The Hidden Life of Garbage* (New York: New York Press, 2005).

Chapter 3: Exercise

1. Bailey, Covert, *The New Fit or Fat* (New York: Houghton-Mifflin Company, 1991), 4.
2. Edward Abbey, *Abbey's Road* (New York: Dutton, 1979).
3. Rowe, Kahn, *Successful Aging* (New York: Random House, 1998).
4. Abrams, John M.D., *Overdosed America* (New York: HarperCollins, 2005), 76.
5. In 2002, an estimated $200 billion was spent on prescription drugs in America. Worldwide, American drug companies sold about twice that amount. This number has risen approximately 300 percent between 1980 and 2000. Cited from: Angell, Marcia M.D., *The Truth about the Drug Companies* (New York: Random House, 2004), xxii.
6. Critser, Greg, *Generation Rx* (New York: Houghton Mifflin, 2005), 2.
7. Goodpaster, Bret H., Brown, Nicholas F., "Skeletal Muscle Lipid and Its Association with Insulin Resistance: What is the Role for Exercise?" *Exercise and Sport Sciences Reviews,* American College of Sports Medicine Series, July 2005, vol. 33, no. 3.
8. This phenomenon is known as EPOC (excess post-exercise oxygen consumption).

Chapter 4: Fit to Serve

1. Abner Hafer, my grandfather, died two months after the writing of this chapter at age ninety-four on August 18, 2005.

Faith & Fitness Magazine
www.faithandfitness.net

The Rodale Institute
www.rodaleinstitute.org

Educational Concerns for Hunger Organization
www.echonet.org

Other Resources from Augsburg

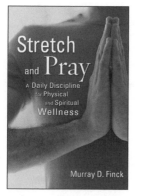

Stretch and Pray by Murray D. Finck
128 pages, 0-8066-5137-7

In this book, Finck provides a step-by-step guide to forty stretches, movements, and postures to improve physical and spiritual well-being. The book features photographs and devotional reflections for individuals to use to create their own routines.

Ending Hunger Now by Bob Dole, George S. McGovern, and Donald E. Messer
128 pages, 0-8006-3782-8

This title brings together three powerful voices behind a shared conviction: that helping the millions who lack basic provision for food has become a religious imperative and human priority. Writing for congregations and individuals of faith, the authors appeal to the religious ethical foundations for action against hunger.

Give Us This Day by Craig L. Nessan
96 pages, 0-8066-4993-3

The author summons the Christian church to listen to the cries of the hungry and commit itself to ending hunger as a matter of status confessionis. Ending hunger is a real possibility for our time. The role of the church in advocating this possibility is crucial.

Available wherever books are sold.